Psalmist,

I Am

*Live through the
many emotions of a
follower, it's OK!*

Ray Abner

WEST BOW
PRESS

A DIVISION OF THOMAS NELSON

WestBow Press books may be ordered through booksellers or by contacting:

WestBow Press
A Division of Thomas Nelson
1663 Liberty Drive
Bloomington, IN 47403
www.westbowpress.com
1-(866) 928-1240

ISBN: 978-1-4497-8680-9 (sc)
ISBN: 978-1-4497-8679-3 (e)
ISBN: 978-1-4497-8681-6 (sc)

Library of Congress Control Number: 2013904506

Printed in the United States of America

WestBow Press rev. date: 4/2/2013

A psalmist. What comes to your mind when you hear that word? Most of us think of David - after all, he was the primary author of Psalms. But if you really think about it, a key reason you associate David with Psalms is perhaps because he was "a man after God's own heart," and the book of Psalms exposes every emotion and struggle of a person passionate for God. From that perspective, anyone who hungers and thirsts for more knowledge of Him, is a psalmist... that includes you!

I have known Ray for over a decade. We have shared many experiences and emotions together: running a marathon, hiking the Grand Canyon rim-to-rim-to-rim, and serving the Lord side by side in many ways. One unwavering and undeniable description of Ray... he is a psalmist! Like David, he possesses a heart to know God and to walk more closely with Him.

Psalmist, I Am is an expression of his personal journey with God. In it, Ray has compiled and categorized some of the key passages of Psalms and arranged them to provide quick nourishment for those in the midst of a divine journey. If you share the struggles, fears, joys, confidence, prayers and faith of an individual who has a heart for God, then you will be greatly encouraged by this well organized book. You will immediately discover that this book is not simply about David, the psalmists, or Psalms. It is about you!

A psalmist... you are!

Dr. Jody Hice
Pastor, The Summit Church, Loganville, GA
Radio Host, The Jody Hice Show, www.WeTalkCulture.com

Since his first involvement on a mission with Kosmos Minitries over six years ago, Ray has been steadfast in working for the Lord. Ray's heart for God is evident in everything he does, including writing his book, **Psalmist, I Am**. Whether he is serving on the mission field in Nicaragua, working alongside others at his local church, or in his private time of study, Ray exemplifies the tone of the psalmists - seeking God through all the seasons and through all the struggles of life.

Matthew Guthas, MDiv
Founder, Kosmos Ministries, Inc.
www.kosmosministries.org
Bethlehem, GA

Psalmist,
I Am

In reading the book of Psalms, one quickly notices the total transparency of the psalmists as they reveal heartfelt emotions. As guided by the Holy Spirit, the psalmists not only relate their feelings, but also reveal great truths about Father God.

Their paths are not indifferent from our lives today! Our days are an ever-changing array of praises and shouts of joy, cries of anguish and pleas for help, acknowledging the goodness of God or questioning the ways of our foes.

Perhaps we are not capturing our thoughts and feelings in writing like the contributors of Psalms did; nevertheless, as sons and daughters of the Most High God, we too are psalmists!

Psalmist, I Am presents emotions and truths found in the book of Psalms. See how your emotions and thoughts of God, as revealed during your journey, align with those of the writers of the Psalms.

Psalmist, I Am simply places verses of Psalms having similar themes into a common chapter. For example, verses containing praise to God can be found in the chapter, "A Psalmist Praises Him." Certainly, any one verse could aptly be associated with more than one "theme", or chapter. This presentation cannot deal with those many possibilities.

Psalmist, I Am will encourage the reader by revealing how much we, today, have in common with the writers of the Psalms!

Ray Abner, a fellow Psalmist!

... loves being a husband and a father, as well as mountain climbing, hiking, long-distance running, cooking and travel. He cherishes his time as a Sunday school teacher, a deacon and participating in short-term missions serving God and His mission. Ray's desire is to remain active both in the local church and with international missions, following a call to utilize the gifts given so freely by Father God. Ray is truly humbled that he was led to complete this work and prays that Christ will be glorified as He uses all things for His greater purpose.

Table of Contents

The God of a Psalmist 2

The Prayer of a Psalmist... 38

A Psalmist in Distress..70

A Psalmist Reveals the Blessed.............................. 98

A Psalmist Exposes the Wicked 112

A Psalmist, a Follower 136

A Psalmist Reveals God's Promises.......................168

A Psalmist Praises Him 188

A Psalmist Points to Christ.....................................216

A Psalmist Recounts God's Ways 230

Psalm Index 249

(Journal pages follow each chapter)

The God of a Psalmist

I and the Father are one. John 10:30 NIV

Who is he,
this King of glory?
The LORD Almighty—
he is the King of glory.
Ps. 24:10 NIV

KING

of

glory

LORD, you are
the God who saves me;
day and night I cry
out to you.
Ps. 88:1 NIV

the

GOD

who

saves

Deliverer …my help and my deliverer;
you are my God
Ps. 40:17 NIV

Stronghold You are God my
stronghold
God, my joy and my
Joy and delight
my Savior and my God.
Delight Ps. 43:2, 4, 5 NIV

a shield around me, my glory,
the One who lifts my head high.
Ps. 3:3 NIV

God is my shield,
who saves the upright in heart.
God is a righteous judge,
and a God who has
indignation every day.
Ps. 7:10-11 NRSV

you are my rock and my fortress
my hope my confidence since
my youth my strong refuge. Your
righteousness, God, reaches to the
heavens, you who have done great
things.
Who is like you, God?
Ps. 71:3, 5, 7, 19 NIV

ROCK
And
FORTRESS

My P
  O
  R
  T
  I
  O
  N

LORD, you alone are my
portion and my cup
Ps. 16:5 NIV

To You, O LORD, I call;
My rock… The LORD is my
strength and my shield.
The LORD is their strength,
And He is a
saving defense to His anointed.
Ps. 28:1, 7, 8 NASB

The LORD is known by his
JUSTICE justice
Ps. 9:16 NLT

Acknowledge that the LORD is God!
He made us, and we are his.
We are his people, the sheep of his
pasture. For the LORD is good.
His unfailing love continues forever,
and his faithfulness continues to each
generation.
Ps. 100:3, 5 NLT

How great are Your works, O LORD!
Your thoughts are very deep.
But You, O LORD,
are on high forever.
Ps. 92:5, 8 NASB

The LORD is my light and my
salvation—whom shall I fear?
The LORD is the stronghold of my
life— of whom shall I be afraid?
Ps. 27:1 NIV

P
R
E
C
I
O
U
S

Your unfailing love, O LORD, is as vast
as the heavens;
your faithfulness reaches beyond the
clouds. Your righteousness is like the
mighty mountains,
your justice like the ocean depths.
You care for people and animals
alike, O LORD. How precious is your
unfailing love, O God!
All humanity finds shelter
in the shadow of your wings.
You feed them from the abundance of
your own house,
letting them drink from your river of
delights. For you are the fountain of
life, the light by which we see
Ps. 36:5-9 NLT

He is the LORD our God;
His judgments are in all the earth.
Ps. 105:7 NASB

The LORD is my shepherd, I lack
nothing.
He makes me lie down in green
pastures, he leads me beside quiet
waters, he refreshes my soul. He
guides me along the right paths for
his name's sake.
Ps. 23:1-3 NIV

He refreshes my SOUL

The LORD looks down from heaven
on humankind
to see if there are any who are wise,
who seek after God.
Ps. 14:2 NRSV

You have commanded your precepts
to be kept diligently.
Ps. 119:4 NRSV

KEPT DILIGENTLY

The sea is his, for he made it,
and his hands formed the dry land.
Ps. 95:5 NIV

my

r
e
f
u
g
e

Truly he is my rock and my salvation;
he is my fortress...
my hope comes from him.
Truly he is my rock and my salvation;
he is my fortress...
he is my mighty rock, my refuge.
God is our refuge.
"Power belongs to you, God,
and with you, LORD, is unfailing love"
Ps. 62:2, 5, 6, 7, 8, 11, 12 NIV

THE
WORLD
STANDS
FIRM

The LORD is king! He is robed in majesty.
Indeed, the LORD is robed in majesty and armed
with strength.
The world stands firm and cannot be shaken.
Your royal laws cannot be changed.
Your reign, O LORD, is holy forever and ever.
Ps. 93:1, 5 NLT

forever

Great are the works of the LORD;
they are pondered by all who delight in them.
Glorious and majestic are his deeds, and his
righteousness endures forever.
The fear of the LORD is the beginning of wisdom; all
who follow his precepts have good understanding.
To him belongs eternal praise.
Ps. 111:2-3, 10 NIV

Who made heaven and earth,
The sea and all that is in them;
Who keeps faith forever;
Who executes justice for the oppressed; Who
gives food to the hungry. The LORD sets the
prisoners free. The LORD opens the eyes of
the blind; The LORD raises up those who are
bowed down; The LORD loves the righteous;
The LORD protects the strangers; He supports
the fatherless and the widow, But He thwarts
the way of the wicked. The LORD will reign
forever, Your God, O Zion, to all generations.
Praise the LORD!
Ps. 146:6-10 NASB

But you, God, see the trouble of the afflicted;
you consider their grief and take it in hand.
you are the helper of the fatherless.
The LORD is King for ever and ever...
You, LORD, hear the desire of the afflicted;
you encourage them, and
you listen to their cry,
defending the fatherless and the oppressed,
so that mere earthly mortals
will never again strike terror.
Ps. 10:14, 16, 17-18 NIV

For the Lord is high above the nations;
his glory is higher than the heavens.
Who can be compared with the Lord our God,
who is enthroned on high?
He stoops to look down on heaven and on earth.
He lifts the poor from the dust
and the needy from the garbage dump.
He sets them among princes, even the princes of his
own people! He gives the childless woman a family,
making her a happy mother.
Praise the Lord!
Ps. 113:4-9 NLT

If the Lord had not been my help,
my soul would soon have lived in the land of silence.
When I thought, "My foot is slipping,"
your steadfast love, O Lord, held me up.
When the cares of my heart are many,
your consolations cheer my soul.
Ps. 94:17-19 NRSV

Though the Lord is exalted, he looks kindly on the
lowly; though lofty, he sees them from afar.
Though I walk in the midst of trouble,
you preserve my life.
You stretch out your hand against the anger of my
foes; with your right hand you save me.
The Lord will vindicate me;
your love, Lord, endures forever—
do not abandon the works of your hands.
Ps. 138:6-8 NIV

"Hear, O My people, and I will admonish you;
O Israel, if you would listen to Me!
"Let there be no strange god among you;
Nor shall you worship any foreign god.
"I, the LORD, am your God,
Who brought you up from the land of Egypt;
Open your mouth wide and I will fill it.
Ps. 81:8-10 NASB

For you bless the righteous, O LORD;
you cover them with favor as with a shield.
Ps. 5:12 NRSV

Truly God is good to Israel,
to those whose hearts are pure.
Those who desert him will perish,
for you destroy those who abandon you.
Ps. 73:1, 27 NLT

You, God, know my folly; my guilt is not
hidden from you.
Ps. 69:5 NIV

If You, LORD, should mark iniquities,
O LORD, who could stand?
But there is forgiveness with You,
That You may be feared.
Ps. 130:3-4 NASB

But the LORD is in his holy Temple;
the LORD still rules from heaven.
He watches everyone closely,
examining every person on earth.
The LORD examines both the righteous and the
wicked.
He hates those who love violence. For the righteous
LORD loves justice. The virtuous will see his face.
Ps. 11:4-5, 7 NLT

Your
Love
is
better
than
LIFE

O God, you are my God
My soul thirsts for you;
my whole body longs for you
in this parched and weary land…
Your unfailing love is better than life itself
you are my helper
your strong right hand holds me securely.
Ps. 63:1, 3, 7, 8 NLT

You are a hiding place for me;
you preserve me from trouble;
you surround me with glad cries of deliverance.
Ps. 32:7 NRSV

He
has
delivered

Behold, God is my helper;
The LORD is the sustainer of my soul.
For He has delivered me from all trouble,
And my eye has looked with satisfaction upon my
enemies.
Ps. 54:4, 7 NASB

...the words of the LORD are flawless,
like silver purified in a crucible,
like gold refined seven times.
Ps. 12:6 NIV

The law of the LORD is perfect,
refreshing the soul.
The statutes of the LORD are trustworthy,
making wise the simple.
The precepts of the LORD are right,
giving joy to the heart.
The commands of the LORD are radiant,
giving light to the eyes.
The fear of the LORD is pure
enduring forever.
The decrees of the LORD are firm,
and all of them are righteous.
They are more precious than gold,
than much pure gold;
they are sweeter than honey,
than honey from the honeycomb.
LORD, my Rock and my Redeemer.
Ps. 19:7-10, 14 NIV

FLAWLESS PERFECT RIGHT

PURE FIRM

I love you, O Lord, my strength.
The Lord is my rock, my fortress, and my deliverer,
my God, my rock in whom I take refuge,
my shield, and the horn of my salvation, my
stronghold.
This God—his way is perfect;
the promise of the Lord proves true;
he is a shield for all who take refuge in him.
For who is God except the Lord?
And who is a rock besides our God?—
The Lord lives! Blessed be my rock,
and exalted be the God of my salvation,
the God who gave me vengeance
and subdued peoples under me;
who delivered me from my enemies;
indeed, you exalted me above my adversaries;
you delivered me from the violent.
Ps. 18:1-2, 30-31, 46-48 NRSV

Lead me in Your truth and teach me,
For You are the God of my salvation;
For You I wait all the day.
Good and upright is the Lord; Therefore He
instructs sinners in the way. He leads the humble in
justice, And He teaches the humble His way.
All the paths of the Lord are lovingkindness and
truth To those who keep His covenant and His
testimonies.
Ps. 25:5, 8-10 NASB

How great is the LORD,
how deserving of praise,
in the city of our God,
which sits on his holy mountain!
We had heard of the city's glory,
but now we have seen it ourselves—
the city of the LORD of Heaven's Armies.
It is the city of our God;
he will make it safe forever.
As your name deserves, O God,
you will be praised to the ends of the earth.
Your strong right hand is filled with victory.
For that is what God is like.
He is our God forever and ever,
and he will guide us until we die.
Ps. 48:1, 8, 10, 14 NLT

we have
seen it

God is our refuge and strength,
A very present help in trouble.
Therefore we will not fear, though the earth
should change
And though the mountains slip into the heart of
the sea; The LORD of hosts is with us;
the God of Jacob is our fortress.
Ps. 46:1-2, 11 NASB

God is
our
Refuge

THE LORD
will
Save me

the LORD will save me
he will hear my voice.
He will redeem me unharmed
from the battle that I wage,
for many are arrayed against me.
Ps. 55:16, 17, 18 NRSV

HE Saved
them

Yet he saved them for his name's sake,
so that he might make known his mighty power.
He rebuked the Red Sea, and it became dry;
he led them through the deep as through a desert.
So he saved them from the hand of the foe,
and delivered them from the hand of the enemy.
Ps. 106:8-10 NRSV

in GOD

we make

our

Boast

You are my King and my God,
who decrees victories for Jacob.
Through you we push back our enemies;
through your name we trample our foes.
I put no trust in my bow,
my sword does not bring me victory;
but you give us victory over our enemies,
you put our adversaries to shame.
In God we make our boast all day long,
and we will praise your name forever.
Ps. 44:4-8 NIV

You, LORD, showed favor to your land;
you restored the fortunes of Jacob.
You forgave the iniquity of your people
and covered all their sins.
You set aside all your wrath
and turned from your fierce anger.
I will listen to what God the LORD says;
he promises peace to his people,
his faithful servants—
but let them not turn to folly.
Surely his salvation is near those who fear him,
that his glory may dwell in our land.
Love and faithfulness meet together;
righteousness and peace kiss each other.
Faithfulness springs forth from the earth,
and righteousness looks down from heaven.
The LORD will indeed give what is good,
and our land will yield its harvest.
Righteousness goes before him
and prepares the way for his steps.
Ps. 85:1-3, 8-13 NIV

He will rescue the poor when they cry to him;
he will help the oppressed, who have no one to
defend them. He feels pity for the weak and the
needy, and he will rescue them.
He will redeem them from oppression and
violence, for their lives are precious to him.
Ps. 72:12-14 NLT

He
will
rescue
the
poor

So
GREAT
is HIS
LOVE

who forgives all your sins
and heals all your diseases,
who redeems your life from the pit
and crowns you with love and compassion,
who satisfies your desires with good things
so that your youth is renewed like the eagle's.
For as high as the heavens are above the earth,
so great is his love for those who fear him; as far
as the east is from the west,
so far has he removed our transgressions from us.
As a father has compassion on his children,
so the LORD has compassion on those who fear
him; for he knows how we are formed,
he remembers that we are dust.
But from everlasting to everlasting
the LORD's love is with those who fear him,
and his righteousness with
their children's children—
with those who keep his covenant
and remember to obey his precepts.
The LORD has established his throne in heaven,
and his kingdom rules over all.
Ps. 103:3-5, 11-14, 17-19 NIV

For the LORD, the Most High, is awesome,
a great king over all the earth.
He subdued peoples under us,
and nations under our feet.
He chose our heritage for us,
the pride of Jacob whom he loves. God is king
over the nations;
God sits on his holy throne.
The princes of the peoples gather
as the people of the God of Abraham.
For the shields of the earth belong to God;
he is highly exalted.
Ps. 47:2-4, 8-9 NRSV

A
W
E
S
O
M
E

All my bones shall say,
'O LORD, who is like you?
You deliver the weak
from those too strong for them,
the weak and needy from those who despoil
them."
Ps. 35:10 NRSV

You
have
delivered
Me

You, LORD, are forgiving and good,
abounding in love to all who call to you.
When I am in distress, I call to you,
because you answer me.
Among the gods there is none like you,
LORD;
no deeds can compare with yours.
For you are great and do marvelous deeds;
you alone are God.
For great is your love toward me;
you have delivered me from the depths,
from the realm of the dead.
But you, LORD, are a compassionate and
gracious God,
slow to anger, abounding in love and
faithfulness.
Give me a sign of your goodness,
that my enemies may see it and be put to
shame,
for you, LORD, have helped me and
comforted me.
Ps. 86:5, 7-8, 10, 13, 15, 17 NIV

O you who answer prayer!
To you all flesh shall come.
When deeds of iniquity overwhelm us,
you forgive our transgressions.
By awesome deeds you answer us with
deliverance,
O God of our salvation;
you are the hope of all the ends of the
earth
and of the farthest seas.
Ps. 65:2-3, 5 NRSV

YOU FORGIVE

Father of orphans and protector of widows
is God in his holy habitation.
God gives the desolate a home to live in;
he leads out the prisoners to prosperity...
Our God is a God of salvation,
and to GOD, the LORD, belongs escape
from death.
Awesome is God in his sanctuary,
the God of Israel;
he gives power and strength to his people.
Blessed be God!
Ps. 68:5-6, 20, 35 NRSV

God has taken his place in the divine council;
in the midst of the gods he holds judgment
Ps. 82:1 NRSV

How lovely is your dwelling place,
O LORD of Heaven's Armies.

A single Day

I long, yes, I faint with longing
to enter the courts of the LORD.
With my whole being, body and soul,
I will shout joyfully to the living God.
A single day in your courts
is better than a thousand anywhere else!
I would rather be a gatekeeper in the house
of my God
than live the good life in the homes of the
wicked.
For the LORD God is our sun and our shield.
He gives us grace and glory.
The LORD will withhold no good thing
from those who do what is right.
Ps. 84:1-2, 10-11 NLT

"I have made a covenant with My chosen;
I have sworn to David My servant,
I will establish your seed forever
And build up your throne to all
generations."
The heavens will praise Your wonders,
O Lord; Your faithfulness also in the
assembly of the holy ones. For who in the
skies is comparable to the Lord?
Who among the sons of the mighty is like
the Lord, A God greatly feared in the
council of the holy ones,
And awesome above all those who are
around Him? O Lord God of hosts, who
is like You, O mighty Lord...
The heavens are Yours, the earth also is
Yours; The world and all it contains, You
have founded them. The north and the
south, You have created them...
You have a strong arm;
Your hand is mighty, Your right hand is
exalted. Righteousness and justice are the
foundation of Your throne;
Lovingkindness and truth go before You.
How blessed are the people who know the
joyful sound!
O Lord, they walk in the light of Your
countenance. Ps. 89:3-8, 11-15 NASB

YOU
founded
the
W
O
R
L
D

25

HE makes springs

P
O
U
R

water

The LORD wraps himself in light as
with a garment;
he stretches out the heavens like a tent
and lays the beams of his upper
chambers on their waters…
He set the earth on its foundations;
it can never be moved.
You covered it with the watery depths
as with a garment;
the waters stood above the mountains.
But at your rebuke the waters fled,
at the sound of your thunder they took
to flight;
they flowed over the mountains,
they went down into the valleys,
to the place you assigned for them.
You set a boundary they cannot cross;
never again will they cover the earth.
He makes springs pour water into the
ravines…
He makes grass grow for the cattle,
and plants for people to cultivate—
bringing forth food from the earth:

wine that gladdens human hearts,
oil to make their faces shine,
and bread that sustains their hearts.
He made the moon to mark the seasons,
and the sun knows when to go down.
How many are your works, LORD!
In wisdom you made them all;
the earth is full of your creatures.
All creatures look to you
to give them their food at the proper
time.
When you give it to them,
they gather it up;
when you open your hand,
they are satisfied with good things.
When you hide your face,
they are terrified;
when you take away their breath,
they die and return to the dust.
When you send your Spirit,
they are created,
and you renew the face of the ground.
Ps. 104:2-3, 5-10, 14-15, 19, 24, 27-30 NIV

O Lord, You have searched me and known *me*.
You know when I sit down and when I rise up;
You understand my thought from afar.
You scrutinize my path and my lying down,
And are intimately acquainted with all my ways.
Even before there is a word on my tongue,
Behold, O Lord, You know it all.
You have enclosed me behind and before,
And laid Your hand upon me.
Such knowledge is too wonderful for me;
It is *too* high, I cannot attain to it.
Where can I go from Your Spirit?
Or where can I flee from Your presence?
If I ascend to heaven, You are there;
If I make my bed in Sheol, behold, You are there.
If I take the wings of the dawn,
If I dwell in the remotest part of the sea,
Even there Your hand will lead me,
And Your right hand will lay hold of me.
If I say, "Surely the darkness will overwhelm
me,

And the light around me will be night,"
Even the darkness is not dark to You,
And the night is as bright as the day.
Darkness and light are alike *to You.*
For You formed my inward parts;
You wove me in my mother's womb.
I will give thanks to You, for I am fearfully
and wonderfully made;
Wonderful are Your works,
And my soul knows it very well.
My frame was not hidden from You,
When I was made in secret,
And skillfully wrought in
the depths of the earth;
Your eyes have seen
my unformed substance;
And in Your book were all written
The days that were ordained *for me,*
When as yet there was not one of them.
How precious also are Your thoughts to
me, O God!
How vast is the sum of them!
If I should count them, they would
outnumber the sand.
When I awake, I am still with You.
Ps. 139:1-18 NASB

I am
fearfully
and wonderfully
made

Your word, LORD, is eternal;
it stands firm in the heavens.
Your faithfulness continues through all generations;
you established the earth, and it endures.
Your laws endure to this day,
for all things serve you.
To all perfection I see a limit,
but your commands are boundless.
Streams of tears flow from my eyes,
for your law is not obeyed.
You are righteous, LORD,
and your laws are right.
The statutes you have laid down are righteous; they
are fully trustworthy.
Hear my voice in accordance with your love;
preserve my life, LORD, according to your laws.
Those who devise wicked schemes are near, but they
are far from your law.
Yet you are near, LORD,
and all your commands are true.
Long ago I learned from your statutes
that you established them to last forever.
All your words are true;
all your righteous laws are eternal.
Ps. 119:89-91, 96, 136-138, 149, 151-152, 160 NIV

The LORD is gracious and merciful;
Slow to anger and great in lovingkindness.
The LORD is good to all,
And His mercies are over all His works.
All Your works shall give thanks to You, O LORD,
And Your godly ones shall bless You.
They shall speak of the glory of Your kingdom
And talk of Your power;
To make known to the sons of men
Your mighty acts
And the glory of the majesty of Your kingdom.
Your kingdom is an everlasting kingdom,
And Your dominion *endures* throughout all
generations.
The LORD sustains all who fall
And raises up all who are bowed down.
The eyes of all look to You,
And You give them their food in due time.
You open Your hand
And satisfy the desire of every living thing.
The LORD is righteous in all His ways
And kind in all His deeds.
The LORD is near to all who call upon Him,
To all who call upon Him in truth.
He will fulfill the desire of those who fear Him;
He will also hear their cry and will save them.
The LORD keeps all who love Him,
But all the wicked He will destroy.
Ps. 145:8-20 NASB

the LORD
SUSTAINS
all who
fall

But you, O LORD, will sit on your
throne forever.
Your fame will endure to every
generation.
You will arise and have mercy on
Jerusalem—
and now is the time to pity her,
now is the time you promised to help.
For your people love every stone in her
walls
and cherish even the dust in her streets.
Then the nations will tremble before
the LORD.

*You will
arise* The kings of the earth will tremble
before his glory.
For the LORD will rebuild Jerusalem.
He will appear in his glory.

*He will
appear* He will listen to the prayers of the
destitute.
He will not reject their pleas.
Ps. 102:12-17 NLT

I know that the LORD is great,
that our LORD is greater than all gods.
The LORD does whatever pleases him,
in the heavens and on the earth,
in the seas and all their depths.
He makes clouds rise from the ends
of the earth;
he sends lightning with the rain
and brings out the wind from his
storehouses.
Your name, LORD, endures forever,
your renown, LORD, through all
generations.
For the LORD will vindicate his
people
and have compassion on his servants.
Ps. 135:5-7, 13-14 NIV

our LORD
is
GREATER
than ALL
gods

You too are a Psalmist! Journal here, with dates…
As you gather your thoughts on how Father God shows
Himself in your life, journal it.
The God of a Psalmist

_____

_____

_____

_____

_____

_____

_____

_____

_____

_____

_____

_____

You too are a Psalmist! Journal here, with dates…
As you gather your thoughts on how Father God shows
Himself in your life, journal it.
The God of a Psalmist

_____

_____

_____

_____

_____

_____

_____

_____

_____

_____

_____

You too are a Psalmist! Journal here, with dates…
As you gather your thoughts on how Father God shows
Himself in your life, journal it.
The God of a Psalmist

_____

_____

_____

_____

_____

_____

_____

_____

_____

_____

_____

You too are a Psalmist! Journal here, with dates...
As you gather your thoughts on how Father God shows
Himself in your life, journal it.
The God of a Psalmist

_____

_____

_____

_____

_____

_____

_____

_____

_____

_____

_____

The Prayer of a Psalmist

First, I thank my God through Jesus Christ...
Romans 1: 8 NIV

Let your steadfast love,
O Lord, be upon us,
even as we hope in you.
Ps. 33:22 NRSV

Hear a just cause, O Lord;
attend to my cry;
give ear to my prayer from
lips free of deceit.
From you let my
vindication come;
let your eyes see the right.
Ps. 17:1-2 NRSV

see

the

RIGHT

Be

E
X
A
L
T
E
D

Have mercy on me, O God,
have mercy…
Be exalted, O God,
above the highest heavens!
May your glory shine over all the earth.
Be exalted, O God, above the
highest heavens.
May your glory
shine over all the earth.
Ps. 57:1, 5, 11 NLT

Be

G
R
A
C
I
O
U
S

May God be gracious to us and bless us
and make his face to shine upon us,
that your way may be known upon earth,
your saving power among all nations.
May God continue to bless us;
let all the ends of the earth revere him.
Ps. 67:1-2, 7 NRSV

Search me, O God,
and know my heart;
test me and know my anxious
thoughts. Point out anything in me
that offends you,
and lead me along the path of
everlasting life.
Ps. 139:23-24 NLT

Lead Me

Break off their fangs, O God!
Smash the jaws of these lions,
O Lord!
May they disappear like water
into thirsty ground.
Make their weapons useless
in their hands.
May they be like snails that
dissolve into slime,
like a stillborn child who will never
see the sun.
Ps. 58:6-8 NLT

may they
be like
snails

Heal Me

As for me, I said, "O LORD, be gracious to
me; heal me, for I have sinned against you."
But you, O LORD, be gracious to me,
and raise me up...
Ps. 41:4, 10 NRSV

Answer me when I call, O God of my
right... Be gracious to me, and hear my
prayer... "O that we might see some good!
Let the light of your face shine on us, O
LORD!"...
Ps. 4:1, 6 NRSV

LISTEN

Give ear to my words, O LORD;
give heed to my sighing.
Listen to the sound of my cry,
my King and my God,
for to you I pray.
Lead me, O LORD, in your righteousness
because of my enemies;
make your way straight before me.
But let all who take refuge in you rejoice;
let them ever sing for joy.
Spread your protection over them...
Ps. 5:1-2, 8, 11 NRSV

...Clear me from hidden faults.
Keep back your servant also
from the insolent;
do not let them have dominion over me.
Then I shall be blameless,
and innocent of great transgression.
Let the words of my mouth and the
meditation of my heart
be acceptable to you...
Ps. 19:12-14 NRSV

O Lord, don't rebuke me in your anger or
discipline me in your rage.
Have compassion on me, Lord, for I am
weak. Heal me, Lord,
for my bones are in agony.
Return, O Lord, and rescue me.
Save me because of your unfailing love.
Ps. 6:1-2, 4 NLT

Rise up, O LORD; O God, lift up your hand;
do not forget the oppressed.
Ps. 10:12 NRSV

Spare my precious Life

Do not stay so far from me,
for trouble is near,
and no one else can help me.
O LORD, do not stay far away!
You are my strength; come quickly to
my aid! Save me from the sword;
spare my precious life from these dogs.
Snatch me from the lion's jaws
and from the horns of these wild oxen.
Ps. 22:11, 19-21 NLT

In times of trouble, may the LORD
answer your cry. May the name of the
God of Jacob keep you safe from all
harm. …May the LORD answer all
your prayers.

Answer our cry

…Answer our cry for help.
Ps. 20:1, 5, 9 NLT

May he vindicate the afflicted of the
people, Save the children of the needy
And crush the oppressor.
Let them fear You while the sun
endures, And as long as the moon,
throughout all generations.
May he come down like rain upon
the mown grass,
Like showers that water the earth.
May his name endure forever;
May his name increase as long as the
sun *shines…*
Ps. 72:4-6, 17 NASB

Save the
children

Deliver me from my enemies, O my
God; protect me from those who rise
up against me. Deliver me from those
who work evil; from the bloodthirsty
save me
…Rouse yourself, come to my help!
Ps. 59:1-2, 4 NRSV

D
E
L
I
V
E
R

ME

come

down

Bow your heavens, O LORD, and come
down...
Stretch out your hand from on high;
set me free and rescue me...
Rescue me from the cruel sword,
and deliver me from the hand of aliens...
Ps. 144:5, 7, 11 NRSV

LORD,
Save me

Arise, LORD, do not let mortals triumph;
let the nations be judged in your presence.
Strike them with terror, LORD;
let the nations know they are only mortal.
Ps. 9:19-20 NIV

rise up

awake

O LORD my God, in you I take refuge;
save me from all my pursuers, and deliver me
Rise up, O LORD, in your anger;
lift yourself up against the fury of my
enemies; awake, O my God...
judge me, O LORD, according to my
righteousness
and according to the integrity that is in me.
O let the evil of the wicked come to an end,
but establish the righteous...
Ps. 7:1, 6, 8-9 NRSV

I call on you, my God, for you will
answer me; turn your ear to me and
hear my prayer.
Show me the wonders of your great
love, you who save by your right hand
those who take refuge in you from
their foes. Keep me as
the apple of your eye…
Rise up, LORD, confront them, bring
them down; with your sword rescue
me from the wicked.
By your hand save me
from such people…
Ps. 17:6-8, 13-14 NIV

Keep me
as the
APPLE
of
Your eye

Pour out your unfailing love on those
who love you;
give justice to those with honest
hearts.
Don't let the proud trample me
or the wicked push me around.
Ps. 36:10-11 NLT

Be good to your servant while I live,
that I may obey your word.
Open my eyes that I may see
wonderful things in your law.
Teach me, LORD, the way of your decrees,
that I may follow it to the end.
Give me understanding, so that I may keep
your law and obey it with all my heart.
Never take your word of truth from my
mouth, for I have put my hope in your laws.
Do good to your servant
according to your word, LORD.
Teach me knowledge and good judgment,
for I trust your commands.
May your unfailing love be my comfort,
according to your promise to your servant.
Let your compassion come to me that I may
live, for your law is my delight.
Uphold me, and I will be delivered;
I will always have regard for your decrees.

Open my
eyes
that I
may
see

doGOOD
toYOUR
SERVANT

Turn to me and have mercy on me, as you
always do to those who love your name.
Direct my footsteps according to your word;
let no sin rule over me.
Make your face shine on your servant
and teach me your decrees.
May my cry come before you, LORD;
give me understanding
according to your word.
May my supplication come before you;
deliver me according to your promise.
May my lips overflow with praise,
for you teach me your decrees.
May my tongue sing of your word,
for all your commands are righteous.
May your hand be ready to help me,
for I have chosen your precepts.
Let me live that I may praise you,
and may your laws sustain me.
I have strayed like a lost sheep.
Seek your servant,
for I have not forgotten your commands.
Ps. 119:17-18, 33-34, 43, 65-66, 76-77, 117,
132-135, 169-173, 175-176 NIV

May my
cry
come
before
You, LORD

Incline
Your
Ear
To
Me

In You, O Lord, I have taken refuge;
Let me never be ashamed.
In Your righteousness deliver me and rescue me;
Incline Your ear to me and save me.
Be to me a rock of habitation to which I may
continually come...
O God, do not be far from me;
O my God, hasten to my help!
Let those who are adversaries of my soul be ashamed
and consumed;
Let them be covered with reproach and dishonor,
who seek to injure me.
And even when I am old and gray, O God, do not
forsake me,
Until I declare Your strength to this generation,
Your power to all who are to come.
Ps. 71:1-3, 12-13, 18 NASB

PARDON
MY
GUILT

do not let me be put to shame;
Be mindful of your mercy, O Lord, and of your
steadfast love, for they have been from of old.
Do not remember the sins of my youth or my
transgressions; according to your steadfast love
remember me, for your goodness' sake, O Lord!
For your name's sake, O Lord, pardon my guilt, for
it is great. Turn to me and be gracious to me,
for I am lonely and afflicted.
May integrity and uprightness preserve me, for I
wait for you.
Redeem Israel, O God, out of all its troubles.
Ps. 25:2, 6-7, 11, 16, 21-22 NRSV

Incline your ear, O LORD, and answer me,
for I am poor and needy.
Preserve my life, for I am devoted to you;
save your servant who trusts in you.
You are my God; be gracious to me, O LORD,
for to you do I cry all day long.
Gladden the soul of your servant,
for to you, O LORD, I lift up my soul.
Teach me your way, O LORD,
that I may walk in your truth;
give me an undivided heart to revere your name.
Show me a sign of your favor,
so that those who hate me may see it and be put
to shame,
because you, LORD, have helped me and
comforted me.
Ps. 86:1-4, 11, 17 NRSV

O LORD, I call upon You; hasten to me!
Give ear to my voice when I call to You!
Do not incline my heart to any evil thing,
To practice deeds of wickedness
With men who do iniquity;
And do not let me eat of their delicacies.
For my eyes are toward You, O God, the LORD; In
You I take refuge; do not leave me defenseless.
Ps. 141:1, 4, 8 NASB

Remember this, O LORD, that the enemy
has reviled, And a foolish people has spurned
Your name. Do not deliver the soul of Your
turtledove to the wild beast;
Do not forget the life of Your afflicted
forever. Consider the covenant;
For the dark places of the land are full of the
habitations of violence. Let not the oppressed
return dishonored; Let the afflicted and
needy praise Your name.
Arise, O God, and plead Your own cause;
Remember how the foolish man reproaches
You all day long. Do not forget the voice of
Your adversaries, The uproar of those who
rise against You which ascends continually.
Ps. 74:18-23 NASB

Vindicate me, O God, and plead my case
against an ungodly nation;

SEND out O deliver me from the deceitful and unjust man!
O send out Your light and Your truth, let

Y   L them lead me; Let them bring me to Your
O   I holy hill And to Your dwelling places.
U   G Ps. 43:1, 3 NASB
R   H
    T

do not turn a deaf ear to me...
Do not drag me away with the wicked-
with those who do evil...
Give them the punishment they so richly
deserve! Measure it out in proportion to
their wickedness. Pay them back for all
their evil deeds! Give them a taste of what
they have done to others.
Save your people! Bless Israel, your special
possession. Lead them like a shepherd, and
carry them in your arms forever.
Ps. 28:1, 3, 4, 9 NLT

pay them BACK

LORD, don't hold back your tender mercies
from me. Let your unfailing love and
faithfulness always protect me. Please,
LORD, rescue me! Come quickly, LORD,
and help me.
may all who seek you rejoice and be glad
in you; But may all who search for you be
filled with joy and gladness in you.
May those who love your salvation
repeatedly shout, "The LORD is great!"
As for me, since I am poor and needy,
let the LORD keep me in his thoughts.
You are my helper and my savior. O my
God, do not delay.
Ps. 40:11, 13, 16-17 NLT

my Helper and my Savior

rescue
me

Arise, O LORD!
Rescue me, my God!
Slap all my enemies in the face!
Shatter the teeth of the wicked!
Ps. 3:7 NLT

"Hear my prayer, O LORD,
and give ear to my cry;
do not hold your peace at my tears. For
I am your passing guest, an alien, like
turn your
gaze
away from
me all my forebears. Turn your gaze away
from me, that I may smile again,
before I depart and am no more."
Ps. 39:12-13 NRSV

Save me, O God,
for the waters have come up to my neck.
Do not let those who hope in you be
put to shame because of me,
O Lord God of hosts;
do not let those who seek you be
dishonored because of me,
O God of Israel.
rescue me from sinking in the mire;
let me be delivered from my enemies
and from the deep waters.
But I am lowly and in pain; let your
salvation, O God, protect me.
Ps. 69:1, 6, 14, 29 NRSV

PROTECT
Me

Do not be silent, O God of my praise.
They say, "Appoint a wicked man
against him; let an accuser stand on
his right.
Help me, O Lord my God!
Save me according to your steadfast love.
Ps. 109:1, 6, 26 NRSV

appoint
a wicked man

Oh, please help us against our enemies,
for all human help is useless.
With God's help we will do mighty things,
for he will trample down our foes.
Ps. 60:11-12 NLT

T   Vindicate me, O Lord,
R   for I have walked in my integrity,
Y me and I have trusted in the Lord without
        wavering.
        Prove me, O Lord, and try me;
T   test my heart and mind.
E   Do not sweep me away with sinners,
S   nor my life with the bloodthirsty
T my But as for me, I walk in my integrity;
HEART redeem me, and be gracious to me.
        Ps. 26:1-2, 9, 11 NRSV

Let your sharp arrows pierce the hearts of
the king's enemies;
let the nations fall beneath your feet.
Ps. 45:5 NIV

O God, do not keep silence;
do not hold your peace or be still, O God!
O my God, make them like whirling dust,
like chaff before the wind.
Fill their faces with shame,
so that they may seek your name, O LORD.
Let them be put to shame and dismayed
forever;
let them perish in disgrace.
Let them know that you alone,
whose name is the LORD,
are the Most High over all the earth.
Ps. 83:1, 13, 16-18 NRSV

Be exalted, O LORD, in your strength...
Ps. 21:13 NRSV

Listen to my prayer, O God.
Do not ignore my cry for help!
Please listen and answer me,
for I am overwhelmed by my troubles.
Confuse them, LORD, and frustrate their
plans...
Let death stalk my enemies;
let the grave swallow them alive...
Ps. 55:1-2, 9, 15 NLT

O God, listen to my cry!
Hear my prayer!
From the ends of the earth,
I cry to you for help
when my heart is overwhelmed.
Lead me to the towering rock of safety
Add many years to the life of the king!
May his years span the generations!
May he reign under God's protection forever.
May your unfailing love and faithfulness watch over
him. Ps. 61:1-2, 6-7 NLT

Let God rise up, let his enemies be scattered;
let those who hate him flee before him.
As smoke is driven away, so drive them away;
as wax melts before the fire,
let the wicked perish before God.
But let the righteous be joyful;
let them exult before God;
let them be jubilant with joy.

Rouse
Yourself,
Lord!

Summon your might, O God;
show your strength, O God, as you have done for us
before.
Ps. 68:1-3, 28 NRSV

Awake!

Rise up

Redeem us

Rouse yourself! Why do you sleep, O Lord?
Awake, do not cast us off forever!
Rise up, come to our help.
Redeem us for the sake of your steadfast love.
Ps. 44:23, 26 NRSV

Be gracious to me, O God, for people
trample on me;
all day long foes oppress me
As they hoped to have my life,
so repay them for their crime;
in wrath cast down the peoples,
O God!
You have kept count of my tossings;
put my tears in your bottle.
Are they not in your record?
Ps. 56:1, 6-8 NRSV

Put my
tears in your
bottle

Be pleased, O God, to deliver me…
But I am poor and needy;
hasten to me, O God!
You are my help and my deliverer;
O Lord, do not delay!
Ps. 70:1, 5 NRSV

*give
light
to my
eyes*

Look on me and answer, LORD my God.
Give light to my eyes, or I will sleep in
death
Ps. 13:3 NIV

O LORD, do not rebuke me in your
anger, or discipline me in your wrath.
Do not forsake me, O LORD;
O my God, do not be far from me;
make haste to help me, O LORD, my
salvation.
Ps. 38:1, 21-22 NRSV

O Lord, come back to us!
How long will you delay?
Take pity on your servants!
Satisfy us each morning with your
unfailing love,
so we may sing for joy to the end of our lives.
Give us gladness in proportion to our former
misery! Replace the evil years with good.
Let us, your servants, see you work again;
let our children see your glory.
And may the Lord our God show us his
approval
and make our efforts successful.
Yes, make our efforts successful!
Ps. 90:13-17 NLT

give
us gladness

Remember me, O Lord, when you show
favor to your people;
help me when you deliver them;
Save us, O Lord our God,
and gather us from among the nations,
that we may give thanks to your holy name
and glory in your praise.
Ps. 106:4, 47 NRSV

Arise, O God, judge the earth!
For it is You who possesses all the
nations.
Ps. 82:8 NASB

Now restore us again, O God of our
salvation.

Put aside

Your

Anger

Against Us

Put aside your anger against us once more.
Will you be angry with us always?
Will you prolong your wrath to all
generations?
Won't you revive us again,
so your people can rejoice in you?
Show us your unfailing love, O Lord,
and grant us your salvation.
Ps. 85:4-7 NLT

O God, restore us
And cause Your face to shine *upon us*, and
we will be saved. O God *of* hosts, restore us
And cause Your face to shine *upon us*, and
we will be saved.
O LORD God of hosts, restore us;
Cause Your face to shine *upon us*, and we
will be saved.
Ps. 80:3, 7, 19 NASB

When I
Call,

Protect me, O God…
Ps. 16:1 NRSV

ANSWER
ME
SPEEDILY

Hear my prayer, O LORD;
let my cry come to you.
Do not hide your face from me in the day
of my distress.
Incline your ear to me;
answer me speedily in the day when I call.
Ps. 102:1-2 NRSV

O LORD God of hosts, hear my prayer;
give ear, O God of Jacob!
Behold our shield, O God;
look on the face of your anointed.
Ps. 84:8-9 NRSV

Pray for peace in Jerusalem.
May all who love this city prosper.
O Jerusalem, may there be peace
within your walls
and prosperity in your palaces.
For the sake of my family and friends,
I will say,
"May you have peace."
For the sake of the house of the LORD
our God,
I will seek what is best for you, O
Jerusalem.
Ps. 122:6-9 NLT

You too are a Psalmist! Journal here, with dates…
You are regularly before Father God with prayers of
thanks, asking for help, seeking wisdom, etc.

The Prayer of a Psalmist

_____

_____

_____

_____

_____

_____

_____

_____

_____

_____

You too are a Psalmist! Journal here, with dates…
You are regularly before Father God with prayers of
thanks, asking for help, seeking wisdom, etc.
The Prayer of a Psalmist

_____

_____

_____

_____

_____

_____

_____

_____

_____

_____

_____

You too are a Psalmist! Journal here, with dates...
You are regularly before Father God with prayers of
thanks, asking for help, seeking wisdom, etc.
The Prayer of a Psalmist

_____

_____

_____

_____

_____

_____

_____

_____

_____

_____

_____

You too are a Psalmist! Journal here, with dates…
You are regularly before Father God with prayers of
thanks, asking for help, seeking wisdom, etc.
The Prayer of a Psalmist

_____

_____

_____

_____

_____

_____

_____

_____

_____

_____

_____

You too are a Psalmist! Journal here, with dates...
You are regularly before Father God with prayers of
thanks, asking for help, seeking wisdom, etc.

The Prayer of a Psalmist

_____

_____

_____

_____

_____

_____

_____

_____

_____

_____

_____

A Psalmist in Distress

So we say with confidence, "The LORD is my helper; I will not be afraid. What can man do to me?" Hebrews 13:6 NIV

Out of the depths I have cried
to You, O LORD.
LORD, hear my voice!
Let Your ears be attentive
To the voice of my
supplications.
If You, LORD, should mark
iniquities,
O LORD, who could stand?
But there is forgiveness with
You,
That You may be feared.
Ps. 130:1-2 NASB

I have
cried to
you,
LORD

My God, my God, why have you forsaken
me? Why are you so far from saving me,
so far from my cries of anguish?
My God, I cry out by day, but you do not
answer, by night, but I find no rest.
But I am a worm and not a man,
scorned by everyone, despised by the people.
All who see me mock me;
they hurl insults, shaking their heads.
"He trusts in the LORD," they say,
"let the LORD rescue him.
Let him deliver him,
since he delights in him."
Ps. 22:1-2, 6-8 NIV

I
cry
out

Your favor, O LORD, made me as secure as a
mountain.
Then you turned away from me, and I was
shattered.
I cried out to you, O LORD.
I begged the LORD for mercy, saying,
"What will you gain if I die,
if I sink into the grave?
Can my dust praise you?
Can it tell of your faithfulness?
Ps. 30:7-9 NLT

What will
You gain
if
I DIE?

The ropes of death entangled me;
floods of destruction swept over me.
The grave wrapped its ropes around me;
death laid a trap in my path.
But in my distress I cried out to the LORD;
yes, I prayed to my God for help...
He rescued me from my powerful enemies,
from those who hated me and were too strong for
me.
They attacked me at a moment when I was in
distress,
but the LORD supported me.
He led me to a place of safety;
he rescued me because he delights in me.
Ps. 18:4-6, 17-19 NLT

With my voice I cry to the LORD;
with my voice I make supplication to the LORD.
I cry to you, O LORD;
I say, "You are my refuge,
my portion in the land of the living."
Give heed to my cry,
for I am brought very low.
Save me from my persecutors,
for they are too strong for me.
Bring me out of prison,
so that I may give thanks to your name.
The righteous will surround me,
for you will deal bountifully with me.
Ps. 142:1, 5-7 NRSV

But as for me, when they were sick,
I wore sackcloth;
I afflicted myself with fasting.
I prayed with head bowed on my bosom,
as though I grieved for a friend or a brother;
I went about as one who laments for a mother,
bowed down and in mourning.
But at my stumbling they gathered in glee,

They
gathered
in glee

they gathered together against me;
ruffians whom I did not know
tore at me without ceasing;
they impiously mocked more and more,
gnashing at me with their teeth.
How long, O Lord, will you look on...
Ps. 35:13-17 NRSV

For my days disappear like smoke,
and my bones burn like red-hot coals.
My heart is sick, withered like grass,
and I have lost my appetite.
Because of my groaning,
I am reduced to skin and bones.
I am like an owl in the desert,
like a little owl in a far-off wilderness.
I lie awake,
lonely as a solitary bird on the roof.
My enemies taunt me day after day.
They mock and curse me.
I eat ashes for food.
My tears run down into my drink
because of your anger and wrath.
For you have picked me up and thrown me
out.
My life passes as swiftly as the evening
shadows.
I am withering away like grass.
Ps. 102:3-11 NLT

I eat
ashes

I am
withering
away

O LORD, rebuke me not in Your wrath,
And chasten me not in Your burning anger.
For Your arrows have sunk deep into me,
And Your hand has pressed down on me.
There is no soundness in my flesh because of
Your indignation;
There is no health in my bones because of
my sin.
For my iniquities are gone over my head; As
a heavy burden they weigh too much for me.
My wounds grow foul *and* fester
Because of my folly.
I am bent over and greatly bowed down;
I go mourning all day long.
For my loins are filled with burning,
And there is no soundness in my flesh.
I am benumbed and badly crushed;
I groan because of the agitation of my heart.
LORD, all my desire is before You;
And my sighing is not hidden from You.

YOUR
arrows have
sunk deep
into
ME

My heart throbs, my strength fails me And
the light of my eyes, even that has gone
from me.
My loved ones and my friends stand aloof
from my plague;
And my kinsmen stand afar off.
Those who seek my life lay snares *for me*;
And those who seek to injure me have
threatened destruction,
And they devise treachery all day long.
But I, like a deaf man, do not hear;
And *I am* like a mute man who does not
open his mouth.
Yes, I am like a man who does not hear,
And in whose mouth are no arguments.
For I am ready to fall,
And my sorrow is continually before me.
For I confess my iniquity;
I am full of anxiety because of my sin.
But my enemies are vigorous *and* strong,
And many are those who hate me
wrongfully.
And those who repay evil for good,
They oppose me, because I follow what is
good.
Ps. 38:1-14, 17-20 NASB

I said, "I will guard my ways
that I may not sin with my tongue;
I will keep a muzzle on my mouth
as long as the wicked are in my presence."
I was silent and still;
I held my peace to no avail;
my distress grew worse, my heart became hot within
me. While I mused, the fire burned...
Surely everyone goes about like a shadow.
Surely for nothing they are in turmoil;
they heap up, and do not know who will gather.
"And now, O LORD, what do I wait for?
My hope is in you.
Deliver me from all my transgressions.
Do not make me the scorn of the fool.
I am silent; I do not open my mouth,
for it is you who have done it.
Remove your stroke from me;
I am worn down by the blows of your hand.
"You chastise mortals
in punishment for sin,
consuming like a moth what is dear to them;
surely everyone is a mere breath.
"Hear my prayer, O LORD,
and give ear to my cry;
do not hold your peace at my tears.
For I am your passing guest,
an alien, like all my forebears.
Turn your gaze away from me, that I may smile
again, before I depart and am no more."
Ps. 39:1-3, 6-13 NRSV

My enemies speak evil against me,
"When will he die, and his name perish?"
And when he comes to see *me*,
he speaks falsehood;
His heart gathers wickedness to itself;
When he goes outside, he tells it.
All who hate me whisper together against me;
Against me they devise my hurt, *saying*,
"A wicked thing is poured out upon him,
That when he lies down,
he will not rise up again."
Even my close friend in whom I trusted,
Who ate my bread,
Has lifted up his heel against me.
Ps. 41:5-9 NASB

even my
close
FRIEND
has lifted up
his heel
against me

As a deer longs for flowing streams,
so my soul longs for you, O God.
My soul thirsts for God,
for the living God.
When shall I come and behold
the face of God?
My tears have been my food
day and night,
while people say to me continually,
"Where is your God?"
These things I remember,
as I pour out my soul:
how I went with the throng,
and led them in procession to the house of God,
with glad shouts and songs of thanksgiving,
a multitude keeping festival.
Why are you cast down, O my soul,
and why are you disquieted within me?
Hope in God; for I shall again praise
him, my help and my God.
My soul is cast down within me;
therefore I remember you

My soul thirsts for YOU

from the land of Jordan and of Hermon,
from Mount Mizar.
Deep calls to deep
at the thunder of your cataracts;
all your waves and your billows
have gone over me.
By day the LORD commands
his steadfast love,
and at night his song is with me,
a prayer to the God of my life.
I say to God, my rock,
"Why have you forgotten me?
Why must I walk about mournfully
because the enemy oppresses me?"
As with a deadly wound in my body,
my adversaries taunt me,
while they say to me continually,
"Where is your God?"
Why are you cast down, O my soul,
and why are you disquieted within me?
Hope in God; for I shall again praise him,
my help and my God.
Ps. 42:1-11 NRSV

For you are God, my only safe haven.
Why have you tossed me aside?
Why must I wander around in grief,
oppressed by my enemies?
Why am I discouraged?

WHY?   Why is my heart so sad…
Ps. 43:2, 5 NLT

But now you have tossed us aside in
dishonor. You no longer lead our armies
to battle. We can't escape the constant
humiliation;

shame is   shame is written across our faces.
written   All we hear are the taunts of our mockers.
across   All we see are our vengeful enemies.
our faces   All this has happened though we have not
forgotten you. We have not violated your
covenant. Our hearts have not deserted you.
We have not strayed from your path.
But for your sake we are killed every day;
we are being slaughtered like sheep.
Why do you look the other way?
Why do you ignore our suffering and
oppression?
We collapse in the dust,
lying face down in the dirt.
Ps. 44:9, 15-18, 22, 24-25 NLT

My thoughts trouble me and I am
distraught because of what my enemy is
saying,
because of the threats of the wicked;
for they bring down suffering on me
and assail me in their anger.
If an enemy were insulting me,
I could endure it;
if a foe were rising against me,
I could hide.
But it is you, a man like myself,
my companion, my close friend,
with whom I once enjoyed sweet fellowship
at the house of God,
as we walked about
among the worshipers.
Evening, morning and noon
I cry out in distress…
My companion attacks his friends;
he violates his covenant.
His talk is smooth as butter,
yet war is in his heart;
his words are more soothing than oil,
yet they are drawn swords.
Ps. 55:2-3, 12-14, 17, 20-21 NIV

His talk is
SMOOTH as
butter,
yet
WAR
is in his heart

How long will you assail a man,
That you may murder *him*, all of you,
Like a leaning wall, like a tottering
fence? Ps. 62:3 NASB
Arrogant foes are attacking me;
RUTHLESS ruthless people are trying to kill me—
PEOPLE people without regard for God.
Ps. 54:3 NIV

Be gracious to us, O Lord, be gracious
to us,
For we are greatly filled with contempt.
Our soul is greatly filled With the
the scoffing of those who are at ease,
PROUD And with the contempt of the proud.
Ps. 123:3-4 NASB

They have set an ambush for me.
Fierce enemies are out
there waiting, LORD,
though I have not sinned or
offended them.
I have done nothing wrong,
yet they prepare to attack me.
Wake up! See what is happening
and help me!
They come out at night,
snarling like vicious dogs
as they prowl the streets.
Listen to the filth that comes from
their mouths;
their words cut like swords.
"After all, who can hear us?"
they sneer.
My enemies come out at night,
snarling like vicious dogs
as they prowl the streets.
They scavenge for food
but go to sleep unsatisfied.
Ps. 59:3-4, 6-7, 14-15 NLT

How long, O LORD?
Will You be angry forever?
Will Your jealousy burn like fire?
Pour out Your wrath upon the
nations which do not know You,
And upon the kingdoms which do
not
call upon Your name.
For they have devoured Jacob
And laid waste his habitation.
Do not remember the iniquities of
our forefathers against us;
Let Your compassion come quickly
to meet us,
For we are brought very low.
Ps. 79:5-8 NASB

they
have
devoured
Jacob

O LORD God of hosts,
How long will You be angry
with the prayer of Your people?
You have fed them
with the bread of tears,
And You have made them to
drink tears in large measure.
You make us an object of
contention to our neighbors,
And our enemies laugh
among themselves.
Ps. 80:4-6 NASB

HOW LONG

I cry aloud to God,
aloud to God, that he may hear me.
In the day of my trouble I seek the LORD;
in the night my hand is stretched out without
wearying;
my soul refuses to be comforted.
Has God forgotten to be gracious?
Has he in anger shut up his compassion?"
Ps. 77:1-2, 9 NRSV

incline
YOUR ear
to MY
cry

Let my prayer come before You;
Incline Your ear to my cry!
For my soul has had enough troubles,
And my life has drawn near to Sheol.
I am reckoned among those who go down to the pit;
I have become like a man without strength,
Forsaken among the dead,
Like the slain who lie in the grave,
Whom You remember no more,
And they are cut off from Your hand.
My eye has wasted away because of affliction;
I have called upon You every day, O LORD;
I have spread out my hands to You.
O Lord, why do You reject my soul?
Why do You hide Your face from me?
You have removed lover and friend far from me;
My acquaintances are *in* darkness.
Ps. 88:2-5, 9, 14, 18 NASB

The snares of death encompassed me;
the pangs of Sheol laid hold on me;
I suffered distress and anguish.
Then I called on the name of the LORD:
"O LORD, I pray, save my life!"
I kept my faith, even when I said,
"I am greatly afflicted";
I said in my consternation,
"Everyone is a liar."
Ps. 116:3-4, 10-11 NRSV

the snares
of
DEATH
encompassed
me

Though hostile nations surrounded me,
I destroyed them all with the authority of the LORD.
Yes, they surrounded and attacked me,
but I destroyed them all with
the authority of the LORD.
They swarmed around me like bees;
they blazed against me like a crackling fire.
But I destroyed them all with
the authority of the LORD.
My enemies did their best to kill me,
but the LORD rescued me.
Ps. 118:10-13 NLT

my eyes
fail,
LOOKING
for YOUR
PROMISE

My soul faints with longing for your salvation,
but I have put my hope in your word.
My eyes fail, looking for your promise;
I say, "When will you comfort me?"
Though I am like a wineskin in the smoke,
I do not forget your decrees.
How long must your servant wait?
When will you punish my persecutors?
The arrogant dig pits to trap me,
contrary to your law.
All your commands are trustworthy;
help me, for I am being persecuted without cause.
They almost wiped me from the earth,
but I have not forsaken your precepts.
In your unfailing love preserve my life,
that I may obey the statutes of your mouth.
Ps. 119:81-88 NIV

my eyes
fail,
while
I wait for
MY GOD

I have sunk in deep mire, and there is no foothold;
I have come into deep waters,
and a flood overflows me.
I am weary with my crying; my throat is parched;
My eyes fail while I wait for my God.
I have become estranged from my brothers
And an alien to my mother's sons.
For zeal for Your house has consumed me,
And the reproaches of those who reproach You have
fallen on me.
Ps. 69:2-3, 8-9 NASB

In my distress I cry to the LORD,
that he may answer me:
"Deliver me, O LORD,
from lying lips,
from a deceitful tongue."
Ps. 120:1-2 NRSV

DELIVER ME,
LORD,
from
lying lips

By the rivers of Babylon—
there we sat down and there we wept when we
remembered Zion.
How could we sing the LORD's song
in a foreign land?
If I forget you, O Jerusalem,
let my right hand wither!
Let my tongue cling to the roof of my mouth,
if I do not remember you,
if I do not set Jerusalem
above my highest joy.
Ps. 137:1, 4-6 NRSV

WE SAT
and
WEPT

Be gracious to me, O LORD,
for I am in distress;
my eye wastes away from grief,
my soul and body also.
For my life is spent with sorrow,
and my years with sighing;
my strength fails because of my misery,
I have   and my bones waste away.
become   I am the scorn of all my adversaries,
like a   a horror to my neighbors,
an object of dread to my acquaintances;
those who see me in the street flee from me.
I have passed out of mind
b v   like one who is dead;
r e   I have become like a broken vessel.
o s   For I hear the whispering of many—
k s   terror all around!—
e e   as they scheme together against me,
n l   as they plot to take my life.
Ps. 31:9-13 NRSV

If only we knew the power
of your anger!
Your wrath is as great as
the fear that is your due.
Teach us to number our days,
that we may gain a heart of
wisdom.
Ps. 90:11-12 NIV

TEACH
US TO
NUMBER
OUR
DAYS

You too are a Psalmist! Journal here, with dates…
Times of struggle and despair can overwhelm us all.
Present your concerns and fears to Him!
A Psalmist in Distress

_____

_____

_____

_____

_____

_____

_____

_____

_____

_____

_____

_____

You too are a Psalmist! Journal here, with dates…
Times of struggle and despair can overwhelm us all.
Present your concerns and fears to Him!

A Psalmist in Distress

_____

_____

_____

_____

_____

_____

_____

_____

_____

_____

_____

You too are a Psalmist! Journal here, with dates…
Times of struggle and despair can overwhelm us all.
Present your concerns and fears to Him!

A Psalmist in Distress

_____

_____

_____

_____

_____

_____

_____

_____

_____

_____

_____

_____

You too are a Psalmist! Journal here, with dates...
Times of struggle and despair can overwhelm us all.
Present your concerns and fears to Him!
A Psalmist in Distress

_____

_____

_____

_____

_____

_____

_____

_____

_____

_____

_____

A Psalmist Reveals
the Blessed

So those who have faith are blessed… Galatians 3:9 NIV

Blessed is the people of
whom this is true;
blessed is the people whose God is the
LORD.
Ps. 144:15 NIV

the
people
whose
GOD
is the
LORD

Blessed are those you choose and
bring near to live in your courts!
We are filled with the good things of
your house, of your holy temple.
Ps. 65:4 NIV

those
YOU
choose

How blessed are those who dwell in
Your house!
They are ever praising You.
How blessed is the man
whose strength is in You,
In whose heart are the highways to Zion!
O Lord of hosts,
How blessed is the man
who trusts in You!
Ps. 84:4-5, 12 NASB

take refuge
in   How blessed are all who take refuge
HIM   in Him! Ps. 2:12 NASB

Then all nations will be blessed
through him,
and they will call him blessed.
Ps. 72:17 NIV

Blessed is the one
who does not walk in
step with the wicked
or stand in the way that
sinners take
or sit in the company of
mockers,
but whose delight is in the law
of the LORD,
and who meditates on his law
day and night. Ps. 1:1-2 NIV

delight
is in the
law

meditates
on His
law

Blessed is the one who comes in the name of the LORD.
We bless you from the house of the LORD.

Ps. 118:26 NRSV

keep
JUSTICE

How blessed are those who keep justice, Who practice righteousness at all times!

Ps. 106:3 NASB

sins
are
COVERED

Blessed is the one
whose transgressions are forgiven,
whose sins are covered.
Blessed is the one
whose sin the LORD does not count against them
and in whose spirit is no deceit.

Ps. 32:1-2 NIV

How blessed is the man who has
made the LORD his trust,
And has not turned to the proud, nor
to those who lapse into falsehood.
Ps. 40:4 NASB

Blessed is the nation whose God is
the LORD,
the people he chose for his
inheritance. Ps. 33:12 NIV

the
NATION
whose
God
is the
LORD

Praise the LORD.
Blessed are those who
fear the LORD,
who find great delight in his
commands.
Their children will be mighty in the
land; the generation of the upright
will be blessed.
Wealth and riches are in their houses,
and their righteousness endures
forever.
Ps. 112:1-3 NIV

He who
considers the
Helpless

How blessed is he who
considers the helpless;
The LORD will deliver him
in a day of trouble.
The LORD will protect him
and keep him alive,
And he shall be called blessed
upon the earth;
And do not give him over
to the desire of his enemies.

the
LORD will
SUSTAIN
him

The LORD will sustain him
upon his sickbed;
In his illness,
You restore him to health.
Ps. 41:1-3 NASB

Behold, children are a gift of the LORD,
The fruit of the womb is a reward.
Like arrows in the hand of a warrior,
So are the children of one's youth.
How blessed is the man whose quiver
is full of them;
They will not be ashamed
When they speak with their enemies
in the gate.
Ps. 127:3-5 NASB

Blessed are those whose
help is the God of Jacob,
whose hope is in the LORD their God.
Ps. 146:5 NIV

by
YOUR favor
our
horn
is
EXALTED

How blessed are the people who know
the joyful sound!
O LORD, they walk in the light of Your
countenance.
In Your name they rejoice all the day,
And by Your righteousness
they are exalted.
For You are the glory of their strength,
And by Your favor our horn is exalted.
For our shield belongs to the LORD,
And our king to the Holy One of
Israel. Ps. 89:15-18 NASB

the
one YOU
discipline,

the
one YOU
teach

Blessed is the one
you discipline, LORD,
the one you teach from your law; you
grant them relief from days of trouble,
till a pit is dug for the wicked.
Ps. 94:12-13 NIV

How blessed are those whose way is
blameless, Who walk in the law of the
LORD. How blessed are those who observe
His testimonies,
Who seek Him with all their heart.
They also do no unrighteousness;
They walk in His ways.
Ps. 119:1-3 NASB

SEEK
HIM

How blessed is everyone who fears the LORD,
Who walks in His ways.
When you shall eat of the
fruit of your hands,

walk in
HIS WAYS

You will be happy and it will be well with
you. Your wife shall be like a fruitful vine
Within your house,
Your children like olive plants
Around your table.
Behold, for thus shall the man be blessed
Who fears the LORD.
The LORD bless you from Zion,
And may you see the prosperity of
Jerusalem all the days of your life.
Indeed, may you
see your children's children.
Peace be upon Israel!
Ps. 128:1-6 NASB

You too are a Psalmist! Journal here, with dates…
God loves to bless His children! As you feel the
blessings of God being poured out on you, journal it.
A Psalmist Reveals the Blessed

_____

_____

_____

_____

_____

_____

_____

_____

_____

_____

_____

_____

You too are a Psalmist! Journal here, with dates…
God loves to bless His children! As you feel the
blessings of God being poured out on you, journal it.

A Psalmist Reveals the Blessed

_____

_____

_____

_____

_____

_____

_____

_____

_____

_____

_____

You too are a Psalmist! Journal here, with dates…
God loves to bless His children! As you feel the
blessings of God being poured out on you, journal it.
A Psalmist Reveals the Blessed

_____

_____

_____

_____

_____

_____

_____

_____

_____

_____

_____

_____

You too are a Psalmist! Journal here, with dates…
God loves to bless His children! As you feel the
blessings of God being poured out on you, journal it.
A Psalmist Reveals the Blessed

_____

_____

_____

_____

_____

_____

_____

_____

_____

_____

_____

_____

A Psalmist Exposes
the Wicked

*Do you not know that the wicked will not inherit
the kingdom of God?* 1 Corinthians 6:9 NIV

The wicked will see this and be
infuriated.
They will grind their teeth in anger;
they will slink away, their hopes
thwarted.
Ps. 112:10 NLT

They are like chaff
that the wind blows away.
the wicked will not stand in the
judgment,
nor sinners in the assembly of the
righteous. Ps. 1:4, 5 NIV

But the one who rules in heaven
laughs. The LORD scoffs at them.
Then in anger he rebukes them,
terrifying them with his fierce fury.
Ps. 2:4-5 NLT

Scoffs
at
them

But as for me, I almost lost my footing.
My feet were slipping, and I was almost gone.
For I envied the proud
when I saw them prosper despite their wickedness.
They seem to live such painless lives;
their bodies are so healthy and strong.

They wear
PRIDE
like a
necklace

They don't have troubles like other people;
they're not plagued with problems like everyone else.
They wear pride like a jeweled necklace
and clothe themselves with cruelty.
These fat cats have everything
their hearts could ever wish for!
They scoff and speak only evil;
in their pride they seek to crush others.
They boast against the very heavens,
and their words strut throughout the earth.
And so the people are dismayed and confused,
drinking in all their words.
"What does God know?" they ask.
"Does the Most High even know what's
happening?"
Look at these wicked people—
enjoying a life of ease while their riches multiply.
Truly, you put them on a slippery path
and send them sliding over the cliff to destruction.
In an instant they are destroyed,
completely swept away by terrors.
When you arise, O LORD,

silly ideas

you will laugh at their silly ideas
as a person laughs at dreams in the morning.
Ps. 73:2-12, 18-20 NLT

But to the wicked God says:
"What right have you to recite my statutes,
or take my covenant on your lips?
For you hate discipline,
and you cast my words behind you.
You make friends with a thief when you
see one, and you keep
company with adulterers.
"You give your mouth free rein for evil,
and your tongue frames deceit.
You sit and speak against your kin;
you slander your own mother's child.
These things you have done and I have
been silent; you thought that I was one just
like yourself.
But now I rebuke you, and lay the charge
before you. Ps. 50:16-21 NRSV

you thought

I

was one
just like
yourself

The enemy is finished, in endless ruins;
the cities you uprooted are now forgotten.
The nations have fallen into the pit they
dug for others.
Their own feet have been caught in the
trap they set. The wicked will go down to
the grave. This is the fate of all the nations
who ignore God.
Ps. 9:6, 15, 17 NLT

nations have
FALLEN
into the pit
they
dug

The idols of the nations are merely things of
silver and gold,
shaped by human hands.
shaped by They have mouths but cannot speak,
human and eyes but cannot see.
hands They have ears but cannot hear,
and noses but cannot smell.
cannot And those who make idols are just like
speak them,
cannot as are all who trust in them.
see Ps. 135:15-18 NLT
cannot
hear For You are not a God who takes pleasure in
wickedness;
No evil dwells with You.
The boastful shall not stand before Your eyes;
You hate all who do iniquity.
You destroy those who speak falsehood;
The LORD abhors the man of bloodshed and
deceit. Ps. 5:4-6 NASB

let them be ashamed who are wantonly
treacherous.
Ps. 25:3 NRSV

See how your enemies growl,
how your foes rear their heads.
With cunning they conspire against your
people; they plot against those you cherish.
"Come," they say, "let us destroy them as a
nation, so that Israel's name is remembered
no more."
With one mind they plot together;
they form an alliance against you–
Ps. 83:2-5 NIV

they plot against
those
YOU
Cherish

Help, LORD, for the godly man ceases to
be,
For the faithful disappear from among the
sons of men. They speak falsehood to one
another;
With flattering lips and with a double
heart they speak. May the LORD cut off all
flattering lips, The tongue that speaks great
things;
Who have said, "With our tongue we will
prevail; Our lips are our own; who is lord
over us?" "Because of the devastation of
the afflicted, because of the groaning of the
needy, Now I will arise," says the LORD;
"I will set him in the safety for which he
longs." Ps. 12:1-5 NASB

Now I
will
ARISE

I have a message from God in my heart
concerning the sinfulness of the wicked:
There is no fear of God
before their eyes.
In their own eyes they flatter themselves
too much to detect or hate their sin.
The words of their mouths are wicked and
they commit deceitful; they fail to act wisely or do good.
themselves Even on their beds they plot evil;
to a they commit themselves to a sinful course
sinful course and do not reject what is wrong.
Ps. 36:1-4 NIV

There is nothing reliable in what they say;
their Their inward part is destruction itself.
throat Their throat is an open grave;
is an They flatter with their tongue.
open Hold them guilty, O God;
grave By their own devices let them fall!
In the multitude of their transgressions
thrust them out,
For they are rebellious against You.
Ps. 5:9-10 NASB

May all my enemies be disgraced and terrified.
May they suddenly turn back in shame.
Ps. 6:10 NLT

They are without pity.   like
Listen to their boasting!   hungry
They track me down and surround me,   lions
watching for the chance to throw me to the
ground.
They are like hungry lions, eager to tear me
apart— like young lions hiding in ambush.
Ps. 17:10-12 NLT

Why do you boast in evil, O mighty man?
The lovingkindness of God endures all day long.
Your tongue devises destruction,
Like a sharp razor, O worker of deceit.
You love evil more than good,   You love evil
Falsehood more than speaking what is right. more than good
You love all words that devour,
O deceitful tongue.
But God will break you down forever;
He will snatch you up and tear you away from
your tent,
And uproot you from the land of the living.
The righteous will see and fear,
And will laugh at him, saying,
"Behold, the man who would not make God his
refuge, But trusted in the abundance of his riches
And was strong in his evil desire."
Ps. 52:1-7 NASB

Do not fret because of those who are evil
or be envious of those who do wrong;
for like the grass they will soon wither,
like green plants they will soon die away.
For those who are evil will be destroyed,
but those who hope in the LORD will
inherit the land.
A little while, and the wicked will be no
more; though you look for them, they will
not be found. The wicked plot against the
righteous and gnash their teeth at them;

the
LORD
   laughs
at the
wicked

but the LORD laughs at the wicked,
for he knows their day is coming.
But the wicked will perish:
Though the LORD's enemies are like the
flowers of the field,
they will be consumed,
they will go up in smoke.
I have seen a wicked and ruthless man
flourishing like a luxuriant native tree, but
he soon passed away and was no more;
though I looked for him,

there will be
no future for
the wicked

he could not be found.
But all sinners will be destroyed;
there will be no future for the wicked.
Ps. 37:1-2, 9-10, 12-13, 20, 35-36, 38 NIV

Why let the nations say,
"Where is their God?"
Our God is in the heavens,
and he does as he wishes.
Their idols are merely things of
silver and gold, shaped by
human hands.
They have mouths but cannot speak,
and eyes but cannot see.
They have ears but cannot hear,
and noses but cannot smell.
They have hands but cannot feel,
and feet but cannot walk,
and throats but cannot make a sound.
And those who make idols are just like them,
as are all who trust in them.
Ps. 115:2-8 NLT

for look, the wicked bend the bow,
they have fitted their arrow to the string,
to shoot in the dark at the upright in heart.
The LORD tests the righteous and the wicked,
and his soul hates the lover of violence.
On the wicked he will rain coals of fire and
sulfur; a scorching wind shall
be the portion of their cup.
Ps. 11:2, 5-6 NRSV

on the
wicked
HE will
rain coals
of
FIRE
and
sulfur

Those who choose another god
multiply their sorrows...
Ps. 16:4 NRSV

O God, insolent people rise up
against me; a violent gang is
trying to kill me.
You mean nothing to them.
Ps. 86:14 NLT

YOU
mean
nothing
to them

How long will you judge unjustly
And show partiality to the wicked?
Vindicate the weak and fatherless;
Do justice to the afflicted and destitute.
Rescue the weak and needy;
Deliver them out of the hand of the wicked.
They do not know nor do they understand;
They walk about in darkness;
All the foundations of the earth are shaken.
I said, "You are gods,
And all of you are sons of the Most High.
"Nevertheless you will die like men
And fall like any one of the princes."
Ps. 82:2-7 NASB

The fool says in his heart,
"There is no God."
They are corrupt, their deeds are vile;
there is no one who does good.
All have turned away, all have become corrupt;
there is no one who does good,
not even one.
Do all these evildoers know nothing?
They devour my people as though eating bread;
they never call on the LORD.
But there they are, overwhelmed with dread,
for God is present in the company of the
righteous.
You evildoers frustrate the plans of the poor,
but the LORD is their refuge.
Ps. 14:1, 3-6 NIV

The
FOOL
says in his heart,
"There is no
God."

the
LORD
will
consume
them

You will capture all your enemies.
Your strong right hand will seize all who hate you.
You will throw them in a flaming furnace
when you appear.
The LORD will consume them in his anger;
fire will devour them.
You will wipe their children from the face of the earth;
they will never have descendants.
Although they plot against you,
their evil schemes will never succeed.
For they will turn and run
when they see your arrows aimed at them.
Ps. 21:8-12 NLT

Because they do not regard the works of the LORD,
or the work of his hands,
he will break them down and build them up no
more. Ps. 28:5 NRSV

YOU
destroyed
them

The kings of the earth joined forces
and advanced against the city.
But when they saw it, they were stunned;
they were terrified and ran away.
They were gripped with terror
and writhed in pain like a woman in labor.
You destroyed them like the mighty ships of
Tarshish
shattered by a powerful east wind.
Ps. 48:4-7 NLT

no one can

R
E
D
E
E
M

Why should I fear when evil days come,
when wicked deceivers surround me—
those who trust in their wealth
and boast of their great riches?
No one can redeem the life of another
or give to God a ransom for them—
the ransom for a life is costly,

the life

no payment is ever enough—

of another

so that they should live on forever
and not see decay.
People, despite their wealth, do not endure;
they are like the beasts that perish.
This is the fate of those who trust in themselves,
and of their followers, who approve their sayings.
Do not be overawed when others grow rich,
when the splendor of their houses increases;
for they will take nothing with them when they die,
their splendor will not descend with them.
Though while they live they

they will

count themselves blessed…

take

Ps. 49:5-9, 12-13, 16-18 NIV

NOTHING
with them
when
they
die

Think again, you fools!
When will you finally catch on?
Is he deaf—the one who made your ears?
Is he blind—the one who formed your eyes?
He punishes the nations—won't he also
punish you?
He knows everything—doesn't he also know
what you are doing?
The LORD knows people's thoughts;
he knows they are worthless!
Who will protect me from the wicked?
Who will stand up for me against evildoers?
Unless the LORD had helped me,
I would soon have settled in the silence of
the grave.
God will turn the sins of evil people back on
them.
He will destroy them for their sins.
The LORD our God will destroy them.
Ps. 94:8-11, 16-17, 23 NLT

I lie down among lions
that greedily devour human prey;   They dug
their teeth are spears and arrows,   a pit in my path -
their tongues sharp swords.
They set a net for my steps;   but they
my soul was bowed down.   have fallen into it
They dug a pit in my path,
but they have fallen into it themselves.
Ps. 57:4, 6 NRSV

They have counseled only to thrust him
down from his high position;
They delight in falsehood;
They bless with their mouth,
But inwardly they curse.   MEN OF
Men of low degree are only vanity and   LOW
men of rank are a lie;   DEGREE
In the balances they go up;
They are together lighter than breath.
Do not trust in oppression
And do not vainly hope in robbery;
If riches increase, do not set your heart
upon them.
Ps. 62:4, 9-10 NASB

The
FOOL
says in his
heart,

"There is no
God."

The fool says in his heart,
"There is no God."
They are corrupt, and their ways are vile;
there is no one who does good.
God looks down from heaven
on all mankind
to see if there are any who understand,
any who seek God.
Everyone has turned away, all have
become corrupt; there is no one who
does good, not even one.
Ps. 53:1-3 NIV

May all who hate Zion
be put to shame and turned backward.
Let them be like the grass on the
housetops that withers before it grows
up, with which reapers do not fill their
hands or binders of sheaves their arms,
while those who pass by do not say,
"The blessing of the LORD be upon you!
We bless you in the name of the LORD!"
Ps. 129:5-8 NRSV

O that you would kill the wicked, O God,
and that the bloodthirsty would depart
from me— those who
speak of you maliciously,
and lift themselves up against you for evil!
Do I not hate those who hate you,
O Lord?
And do I not loathe those who rise up
against you?
I hate them with perfect hatred;   Perfect hatred
I count them my enemies.
Ps. 139:19-22 NRSV

For my enemies have spoken against me;   My
And those who watch for my life have   Enemies
consulted together,   Have
Saying, "God has forsaken him;   Spoken
Pursue and seize him, for there is no one to   Against
deliver." Ps. 71:10-11 NASB   Me

But you have rejected all who stray from
your decrees.   scum
They are only fooling themselves.
You skim off the wicked of the earth like
scum; no wonder I love to obey your laws!
Ps. 119:118-119 NLT

Hear my voice, O God, in my complaint;
preserve my life from the dread enemy.
Hide me from the secret plots of the wicked,
from the scheming of evildoers,
who whet their tongues like swords,
who aim bitter words like arrows,
shooting from ambush at the blameless;
they shoot suddenly and without fear.
They hold fast to their evil purpose;
they talk of laying snares secretly,
thinking, "Who can see us?
Who can search out our crimes?
We have thought out a
cunningly conceived plot."
For the human heart and mind are deep.
Ps. 64:1-6 NRSV

tongues
like
swords

Surely God will shatter the
head of His enemies,
The hairy crown of him who goes on in his
guilty deeds. The LORD said, "I will bring
them back from Bashan. I will bring them
back from the depths of the sea;
That your foot may shatter them in blood,
The tongue of your dogs may have its
portion from your enemies."
Ps. 68:21-23 NASB

The wicked will not rule the land of the
godly, for then the godly
might be tempted to do wrong.
O Lord, do good to those who are good,
whose hearts are in tune with you.
But banish those who turn to crooked
ways, O Lord. Take them away with those
who do evil. May Israel have peace!
Ps. 125:3-5 NLT

Do you rulers indeed speak justly?
Do you judge people with equity?
No, in your heart you devise injustice,
and your hands mete out
violence on the earth.
Even from birth the wicked go astray;
from the womb they are wayward,
spreading lies.
The righteous will be glad
when they are avenged,
when they dip their feet in the blood of the
wicked. Then people will say,   surely there
"Surely the righteous still are rewarded;   is a God
surely there is a God who judges the earth." who judges
Ps. 58:1-3, 10-11 NIV   the earth

You too are a Psalmist! Journal here, with dates…
The ways of the wicked could affect our relationship
with Him. Journal your thoughts and experiences.

A Psalmist Exposes the Wicked

_____

_____

_____

_____

_____

_____

_____

_____

_____

_____

_____

_____

You too are a Psalmist! Journal here, with dates...
The ways of the wicked could affect our relationship
with Him. Journal your thoughts and experiences.

A Psalmist Exposes the Wicked

_____

_____

_____

_____

_____

_____

_____

_____

_____

_____

_____

_____

You too are a Psalmist! Journal here, with dates…
The ways of the wicked could affect our relationship
with Him. Journal your thoughts and experiences.
A Psalmist Exposes the Wicked

_____

_____

_____

_____

_____

_____

_____

_____

_____

_____

_____

_____

You too are a Psalmist! Journal here, with dates…
The ways of the wicked could affect our relationship
with Him. Journal your thoughts and experiences.
A Psalmist Exposes the Wicked

_____

_____

_____

_____

_____

_____

_____

_____

_____

_____

_____

A Psalmist, a Follower

"Come, follow me," Jesus said... Mark 1:17 NIV

I know you are pleased
with me,
for you have not let my
enemies triumph over me.
You have preserved my life
because I am innocent;
you have brought me into
your presence forever.
Ps. 41:11-12 NLT

YOUR
PRESENCE
FOREVER

For you, O LORD, are my hope,
my trust, O LORD, from my youth.
Upon you I have leaned from my birth;
it was you who took me from my mother's womb.
My praise is continually of you.
I have been like a portent to many,
but you are my strong refuge.
My mouth is filled with your praise,
and with your glory all day long.
But I will hope continually,
and will praise you yet more and more.
My mouth will tell of your righteous acts,
of your deeds of salvation all day long,
though their number is past my knowledge.
I will come praising the mighty deeds of the LORD
God, I will praise your righteousness, yours alone.
O God, from my youth you have taught me,
and I still proclaim your wondrous deeds.
I will also praise you with the harp
for your faithfulness, O my God;
I will sing praises to you with the lyre,
O Holy One of Israel.
My lips will shout for joy
when I sing praises to you;
my soul also, which you have rescued.
All day long my tongue will talk of your righteous
help, for those who tried to do me harm
have been put to shame, and disgraced.
Ps. 71:5-8, 14-17, 22-24 NRSV

My mouth will tell

I say to the LORD, "You are my LORD;
I have no good apart from you."
As for the holy ones in the land,
they are the noble,
in whom is all my delight.
The LORD is my chosen portion and my cup;
you hold my lot.
The boundary lines have fallen
for me in pleasant places;
I have a goodly heritage.
Ps. 16:2-3, 5-6 NRSV

YOU
are my
LORD

Who may ascend into the hill of the LORD? And
who may stand in His holy place? He who has
clean hands and a pure heart,
Who has not lifted up his soul to falsehood And
has not sworn deceitfully. He shall receive a
blessing from the LORD And righteousness from
the God of his salvation.
This is the generation of those who seek Him,
Who seek Your face—even Jacob.
Ps. 24:3-6 NASB

I do not spend time with liars
or go along with hypocrites.
I hate the gatherings of those who do evil,
and I refuse to join in with the wicked.
I wash my hands to declare my innocence.
I come to your altar, O LORD,
singing a song of thanksgiving
and telling of all your wonders.
Ps. 26:4-7 NLT

I trust in
the
LOVING-
KINDNESS
of God

But as for me, I am like a green olive
tree in the house of God; I trust in the
lovingkindness of God forever and ever.
I will give You thanks forever, because You
have done it, And I will wait on Your name,
for it is good, in the presence of
Your godly ones.
Ps. 52:8-9 NASB

We ponder your steadfast love, O God,

We ponder
your
steadfast
love

in the midst of your temple. Ps. 48:9 NRSV

like a tree planted by streams of water,
which yields its fruit in season
and whose leaf does not wither—
whatever they do prospers.
Ps. 1:3 NIV

The one whose walk is blameless, who does
what is righteous,
who speaks the truth from their heart;
whose tongue utters no slander,
who does no wrong to a neighbor,
and casts no slur on others;
who despises a vile person
but honors those who fear the LORD; who
keeps an oath even when it hurts,
and does not change their mind; who lends
money to the poor without interest;
who does not accept a bribe
against the innocent.   will
Whoever does these things   never be shaken
will never be shaken.
Ps. 15:2-5 NIV

When I kept silent about my sin,
my body wasted away
Through my groaning all day long.
For day and night Your hand was heavy upon me;
My vitality was drained away as with the fever heat

YOU
FORGAVE
the guilt
of my sin

of summer. I acknowledged my sin to You,
And my iniquity I did not hide;
I said, "I will confess my transgressions to the
LORD"; And You forgave the guilt of my sin.
Ps. 32:3-5 NASB

Like our ancestors, we have sinned.
We have done wrong! We have acted wickedly!
Our ancestors in Egypt
were not impressed by the LORD's miraculous deeds.
They soon forgot his many acts of kindness to them.
Instead, they rebelled against him at the Red Sea.
Ps. 106:6-7 NLT

But I am a worm, and not human;
scorned by others, and despised by the people.
All who see me mock at me;
they make mouths at me, they shake their
heads; "Commit your cause to the LORD; let him
deliver— let him rescue the one in whom he
delights!" Yet it was you who took me from the
womb; you kept me safe on my mother's breast.

YOU have
been my
GOD

On you I was cast from my birth,
and since my mother bore me you have been my
God. Ps. 22:6-10 NRSV

Out of my distress I called on the LORD;
the LORD answered me and set me in a broad
place.
With the LORD on my side I do not fear.
What can mortals do to me?
The LORD is on my side to help me;
I shall look in triumph on those who hate me.
It is better to take refuge in the LORD
than to put confidence in mortals.
It is better to take refuge in the LORD
than to put confidence in princes.
Ps. 118:5-9 NRSV

*take refuge in
the LORD*

To You, O LORD, I lift up my soul.
O my God, in You I trust,
Do not let me be ashamed;
Do not let my enemies exult over me.
Indeed, none of those who wait for You will be
ashamed;
Those who deal treacherously without cause will
be ashamed. Lead me in Your truth and teach me,
For You are the God of my salvation;
For You I wait all the day. Who is the man who
fears the LORD? He will instruct him in the way
he should choose.
His soul will abide in prosperity,
And his descendants will inherit the land.
The secret of the LORD is for those who fear Him,
And He will make them know His covenant.
My eyes are continually toward the LORD,
For He will pluck my feet out of the net.
Ps. 25:1-3, 5, 12-15 NASB

the LORD supported me.
He led me to a place of safety;
he rescued me because he delights in me.
The LORD rewarded me for doing right;
he restored me because of my innocence.
For I have kept the ways of the LORD;
I have not turned from my God to follow evil.
Ps. 18:18-21 NLT

Be still

wait
patiently
for HIM

Trust in the LORD, and do good;
so you will live in the land, and enjoy security.
Take delight in the LORD,
and he will give you the desires of your heart.
Commit your way to the LORD;
trust in him, and he will act.
He will make your vindication shine like the light,
and the justice of your cause like the noonday.
Be still before the LORD, and wait patiently for him;
do not fret over those who prosper in their way,
over those who carry out evil devices.
Our steps are made firm by the LORD,
when he delights in our way;
though we stumble, we shall not fall headlong,
for the LORD holds us by the hand.
Ps. 37:3-7, 23-24 NRSV

Our soul waits for the LORD;
he is our help and shield.
Our heart is glad in him,
because we trust in his holy name.
Ps. 33:20-21 NRSV

Our soul waits

But I will trust in You.
Ps. 55:23 NASB

Don't put your confidence in powerful
people;
there is no help for you there. When they
breathe their last, they return to the earth,
and all their plans die with them.
Ps. 146:3-4 NLT

Oh, that my ways were steadfast
in obeying your decrees!
Then I would not be put to shame
when I consider all your commands.
I will praise you with an upright heart
as I learn your righteous laws.
I will obey your decrees…
Your statutes are my delight;
they are my counselors.
I will always obey your law,
for ever and ever.
I will walk about in freedom,
for I have sought out your precepts.
I will speak of your statutes before kings
and will not be put to shame,
for I delight in your commands
because I love them.
The law from your mouth is more precious
to me
than thousands of pieces of silver and gold.
If your law had not been my delight,
I would have perished in my affliction.
I will never forget your precepts,
for by them you have preserved my life.
Oh, how I love your law!
I meditate on it all day long.
Your commands are always with me

I delight
in your
commands
because I love
them

and make me wiser than my enemies.
I have more insight than all my teachers,
for I meditate on your statutes.
I have more understanding than the elders,
for I obey your precepts.
I have kept my feet from every evil path
so that I might obey your word.
I open my mouth and pant,
longing for your commands.
I rejoice in your promise
like one who finds great spoil.
I hate and detest falsehood
but I love your law.
Seven times a day I praise you
for your righteous laws.
Great peace have those who love your law,
and nothing can make them stumble.
I wait for your salvation, LORD,
and I follow your commands.
I obey your statutes,
for I love them greatly.
I obey your precepts and your statutes,
for all my ways are known to you.
I long for your salvation, LORD,
and your law gives me delight.
Ps. 119:5-8, 24, 44-47, 72, 92-93, 97-101,
131, 162-168, 174 NIV

I pant,
longing
for your
commands

I wait for your
salvation

Those who look to him for help will be
radiant with joy;
no shadow of shame will darken their faces.
In my desperation I prayed,

TASTE
and the Lord listened;
and
he saved me from all my troubles.
SEE
For the angel of the Lord is a guard;
that the
he surrounds and
Lord
defends all who fear him.
is
Taste and see that the Lord is good.
GOOD
Oh, the joys of those who take refuge in
him! The eyes of the Lord watch over those
who do right;
his ears are open to their cries for help.
The Lord is close to the brokenhearted;
he rescues those whose spirits are crushed.
The righteous person faces many troubles,
but the Lord comes to
the rescue each time.
For the Lord protects the bones of the
righteous; not one of them is broken!
But the Lord will redeem
those who serve him.
No one who takes refuge in him will be
condemned.
Ps. 34:5-8, 15, 18-20, 22 NLT

When evildoers came upon me to devour
my flesh, My adversaries and my enemies,
they stumbled and fell.
Though a host encamp against me,   YOUR
My heart will not fear;   FACE
Though war arise against me,   LORD
In spite of this I shall be confident. When
You said, "Seek My face," my heart said to   I SHALL
You, "Your face, O LORD, I shall seek."   SEEK
For my father and my mother have
forsaken me, But the LORD will take me
up. I would have despaired unless I had
believed that I would
see the goodness of the LORD
In the land of the living.
Wait for the LORD; Be strong and let your
heart take courage; Yes, wait for the LORD.
Ps. 27:2-3, 8, 10, 13-14 NASB   I
                                                    WAIT
                                                    for the
I wait for the LORD, my soul does wait,   LORD
And in His word do I hope.
My soul waits for the LORD
More than the watchmen for the morning;
Indeed, more than the watchmen for the
morning. O Israel, hope in the LORD;
For with the LORD there is lovingkindness,
And with Him is abundant redemption.
Ps. 130:5-7 NASB

O God, you are my God, I seek you,
my soul thirsts for you;
my flesh faints for you,
as in a dry and weary land where there is no
water. So I will bless you as long as I live;
I will lift up my hands and call on your
name.
My soul is satisfied as with a rich feast, and
my mouth praises you with joyful lips
when I think of you on my bed,
and meditate on you in the
watches of the night;
for you have been my help,
and in the shadow of your
wings I sing for joy.
My soul clings to you;
your right hand upholds me.
Ps. 63:1, 4-8 NRSV

My soul
thirsts for
YOU

I waited patiently for the LORD to help me,
and he turned to me and heard my cry.
He has given me a new song to sing,
a hymn of praise to our God.
Many will see what he has done
and be amazed.
They will put their trust in the LORD.
I take joy in doing your will, my God,
for your instructions are written on my heart."
I have told all your people
about your justice.
I have not been afraid to speak out,
as you, O LORD, well know.
I have not kept the good news of your
justice hidden in my heart;
I have talked about your faithfulness and
saving power.
I have told everyone in the great assembly
of your unfailing love and faithfulness.
Ps. 40:1, 3, 8-10 NLT

For I know my transgressions,
and my sin is ever before me.
Against you, you alone, have I sinned,
and done what is evil in your sight,
so that you are justified in your sentence
and blameless when you pass judgment.
Indeed, I was born guilty,
a sinner when my mother conceived me.

YOU
Desire
Truth

You desire truth in the inward being;
therefore teach me wisdom
in my secret heart.
Ps. 51:3-6 NRSV

You have tried my heart;
You have visited me by night;
You have tested me and You find nothing;
I have purposed that
my mouth will not transgress.
As for the deeds of men,
by the word of Your lips.

my steps
have
held fast
to
Your paths

I have kept from the paths of the violent.
My steps have held fast
to Your paths.
My feet have not slipped.
As for me, I shall behold
Your face in righteousness;
I will be satisfied with Your likeness when
I awake. Ps. 17:3-5, 15 NASB

I shall sing of Your strength;
Yes, I shall joyfully sing of Your
lovingkindness…
Ps. 59:16 NASB

From the end of the earth I call to
you, when my heart is faint.
Lead me to the rock
that is higher than I;
Let me abide in your tent forever,
find refuge under the shelter of your
wings.
So I will always sing praises to your
name,
as I pay my vows day after day.
Ps. 61:2, 4, 8 NRSV

I look to you for protection.
I will hide beneath the shadow of your
wings until the danger passes by.
I cry out to God Most High,
to God who will fulfill his purpose for me.
My heart is confident in you, O God;

my heart is
confident

my heart is confident.
No wonder I can sing your praises!
Wake up, my heart! Wake up, O lyre and
harp! I will wake the dawn with my song.
Ps. 57:1-2, 7-8 NLT

when I am afraid, I put my trust in you.
In God, whose word I praise,
in God I trust; I am not afraid;
what can flesh do to me?

In God
I trust

In God, whose word I praise,
in the LORD, whose word I praise,
in God I trust; I am not afraid.
What can a mere mortal do to me?
My vows to you I must perform, O God;
I will render thank offerings to you.
For you have delivered my soul from death,
and my feet from falling,
so that I may walk before God
in the light of life.
Ps. 56:3-4, 10-13 NRSV

He only is my rock and my salvation,
My stronghold; I shall not be greatly shaken.
My soul, wait in silence for God only,
For my hope is from Him.
He only is my rock and my salvation,
My stronghold; I shall not be shaken.
On God my salvation and my glory rest;
The rock of my strength, my refuge is in God.
Trust in Him at all times, O people;
Pour out your heart before Him;
God is a refuge for us. Ps. 62:2, 5-8 NASB

On God my
salvation
and my glory
rest

O my people, listen to my instructions.
Open your ears to what I am saying,
for I will speak to you in a parable.
I will teach you hidden lessons from our past—
stories we have heard and known,
stories our ancestors handed down to us.
We will not hide these truths from our children;
we will tell the next generation
about the glorious deeds of the LORD,
about his power and his mighty wonders.
For he issued his laws to Jacob;
he gave his instructions to Israel.
He commanded our ancestors
to teach them to their children,
so the next generation might know them—
even the children not yet born—
and they in turn will teach their own children.
So each generation should set its hope anew on God,
not forgetting his glorious miracles
and obeying his commands.
Then they will not be like their ancestors—
stubborn, rebellious, and unfaithful,
refusing to give their hearts to God.
Ps. 78:1-8 NLT

We have heard with our ears, O God,
our ancestors have told us,
what deeds you performed in their days,
in the days of old:
you with your own hand
drove out the nations,
but them you planted;
you afflicted the peoples,
but them you set free;
for not by their own sword did they win
the land, nor did their own arm give them
victory; but your right hand, and your arm,
and the light of your countenance,
for you delighted in them.
Ps. 44:1-3 NRSV

When the LORD brought back his exiles to
Jerusalem,
it was like a dream!
We were filled with laughter,
the   and we sang for joy.
LORD   And the other nations said,
has done   "What amazing things the LORD has done
amazing   for them."
things   Yes, the LORD has done amazing things for
us! What joy!
Ps. 126:1-3 NLT

This will be written for the
generation to come,
That a people yet to be created may praise
the Lord. For He looked down from His
holy height; From heaven the Lord gazed
upon the earth, To hear the groaning of
the prisoner,
To set free those who were doomed to death,
That *men* may tell of the name of the Lord
in Zion And His praise in Jerusalem,
When the peoples are gathered together,
And the kingdoms, to serve the Lord.
He has weakened my strength in the way;
He has shortened my days.
I say, "O my God, do not take me away
in the midst of my days, Your years are
throughout all generations. "The children
of Your servants will continue, And their
descendants will be established before You."
Ps. 102:18-24, 28 NASB

Those who trust in the Lord are like
Mount Zion, which cannot be moved, but
abides forever. As the mountains surround
Jerusalem, so the Lord surrounds his people,
from this time on and forevermore.
Ps. 125:1-2 NRSV

The Lord
surrounds
His people

Light arises in the darkness for the upright;
He is gracious and
compassionate and righteous.
It is well with the man
who is gracious and lends;
He will maintain his cause in judgment.
For he will never be shaken;
The righteous will be remembered forever.
He will not fear evil tidings;
His heart is steadfast, trusting in the Lord.
His heart is upheld, he will not fear,
Until he looks with satisfaction on his
adversaries.
He has given freely to the poor,
His righteousness endures forever;
His horn will be exalted in honor.
Ps. 112:4-9 NASB

OUR
HISTORY

The godly will see these things and be glad,
while the wicked are struck silent.
Those who are wise will take all this to heart;
they will see in our history the faithful love
of the LORD. Ps. 107:42-43 NLT

Whom have I in heaven but you?
And there is nothing on earth that I desire other
than you.
My flesh and my heart may fail,
but God is the strength of my heart and my
portion forever.
Indeed, those who are far from you will perish;
you put an end to those who are false to you.
But for me it is good to be near God;
I have made the LORD GOD my refuge,
to tell of all your works.
Ps. 73:25-28 NRSV

Whom have I in
heaven but YOU?

Then I will praise God's name with singing,
and I will honor him with thanksgiving.
For this will please the LORD more than
sacrificing cattle, more than presenting a bull with
its horns and hooves. The humble will see their
God at work and be glad. Let all who seek God's
help be encouraged.
For the LORD hears the cries of the needy;
he does not despise his imprisoned people.
Praise him, O heaven and earth,
the seas and all that move in them.
For God will save Jerusalem
and rebuild the towns of Judah.
His people will live there
and settle in their own land.

I will praise God's
name with singing

The descendants of those who obey him will
inherit the land,
and those who love him will live there in safety.
Ps. 69:30-36 NLT

I will
sing to the
LORD
as long as
I live

I will sing to the LORD
as long as I live;
I will sing praise to my
God while I have being.
May my meditation be pleasing to him,
for I rejoice in the LORD.
Let sinners be consumed from the earth,
and let the wicked be no more…
Ps. 104:33-35 NRSV

Willingly I will sacrifice to You;
I will give thanks to Your name, O
LORD, for it is good.
Ps. 54:6 NASB

It is
GOOD

May the LORD give you increase,
both you and your children.
May you be blessed by the LORD,
who made heaven and earth.
The heavens are the LORD's heavens,
but the earth he has given to human
beings.
The dead do not praise the LORD,
nor do any that go down into silence.
But we will bless the LORD
from this time on and forevermore.
Praise the LORD! Ps. 115:14-18 NRSV

may you be blessed by the LORD

LORD, my heart is not proud;
my eyes are not haughty.
I don't concern myself
with matters too great
or too awesome for me to grasp.
Instead, I have calmed and quieted myself,
like a weaned child who no longer cries for
its mother's milk.
Yes, like a weaned child is
my soul within me.
O Israel, put your hope in the LORD—
now and always.
Ps. 131:1-3 NLT

put your HOPE in the LORD

How very good and pleasant it is
when kindred live together in unity!
It is like the precious oil on the head,
running down upon the beard,
on the beard of Aaron,
running down over
the collar of his robes.
It is like the dew of Hermon,

The
which falls on the

LORD
mountains of Zion.

ordained
For there the LORD

His blessing,
ordained his blessing,

LIFE
life forevermore.

forevermore
Ps. 133:1-3 NRSV

You too are a Psalmist! Journal here, with dates...
You are a child of God and are certain of your future in
Him! Write of your ways and the truths you enjoy.
A Psalmist, a Follower

_____

_____

_____

_____

_____

_____

_____

_____

_____

_____

_____

_____

You too are a Psalmist! Journal here, with dates...
You are a child of God and are certain of your future in
Him! Write of your ways and the truths you enjoy.
A Psalmist, a Follower

_____

_____

_____

_____

_____

_____

_____

_____

_____

_____

_____

You too are a Psalmist! Journal here, with dates…
You are a child of God and are certain of your future in
Him! Write of your ways and the truths you enjoy.
A Psalmist, a Follower

You too are a Psalmist! Journal here, with dates…
You are a child of God and are certain of your future in
Him! Write of your ways and the truths you enjoy.
A Psalmist, a Follower

_____

_____

_____

_____

_____

_____

_____

_____

_____

_____

_____

_____

You too are a Psalmist! Journal here, with dates...
You are a child of God and are certain of your future in
Him! Write of your ways and the truths you enjoy.
A Psalmist, a Follower

_____

_____

_____

_____

_____

_____

_____

_____

_____

_____

_____

_____

A Psalmist Reveals
God's Promises

*For no matter how many promises God has made, they
are "Yes" in Christ…* 2 Corinthians 1:20 NIV

Now I know that the LORD
saves His anointed;
He will answer him from
His holy heaven
With the saving strength
of His right hand.
Ps. 20:6 NASB

I shall
live
for
HIM

All the ends of the earth shall remember
and turn to the LORD;
and all the families of the nations
shall worship before him.
For dominion belongs to the LORD,
and he rules over the nations.
To him, indeed, shall all who sleep in the earth
bow down; before him shall bow all who go
down to the dust, and I shall live for him.
Posterity will serve him;
future generations will be told about the LORD,
and proclaim his deliverance to a people yet
unborn, saying that he has done it.
Ps. 22:27-31 NRSV

ALL...
will come
and
WORSHIP

All the nations you have made
will come and worship before you, LORD;
they will bring glory to your name.
Ps. 86:9 NIV

THEY...
Will declare
the work of
GOD

Then all men will fear,
And they will declare the work of God,
And will consider what He has done.
The righteous man will be glad
in the LORD
and will take refuge in Him;
And all the upright in heart will glory.
Ps. 64:9-10 NASB

You can be sure of this:
The LORD set apart the godly for himself.
The LORD will answer when I call to him.
In peace I will lie down and sleep,
for you alone, O LORD, will keep me safe.
Ps. 4:3, 8 NLT

The
LORD
Will
Answer

For I hope in You, O LORD;
You will answer, O LORD my God.
Ps. 38:15 NASB

You
Will
Answer

The LORD has heard my plea;
the LORD will answer my prayer.
Ps. 6:9 NLT

The
LORD
Has heard

I cry aloud to the LORD,
and he answers me from his holy hill.
I lie down and sleep;
I wake again, for the LORD sustains me.
Deliverance belongs to the LORD...
Ps. 3:4-5, 8 NRSV

He
answers me

God will
ransom
my soul

But God will ransom my soul
from the power of Sheol,
for he will receive me.
Ps. 49:15 NRSV

I will enter
YOUR house

But as for me, by Your abundant
lovingkindness I will enter Your
house, At Your holy temple I will
bow in reverence for You.
Ps. 5:7 NASB

HIS
FACE

The upright will behold His face.
Ps. 11:7 NASB

Even though I walk
through the darkest valley,
I will fear no evil,
for you are with me;   YOU are
your rod and your staff,   with me
they comfort me.
You prepare a table before me
in the presence of my enemies.
You anoint my head with oil;
my cup overflows.
Surely your goodness and love will
follow me
all the days of my life,
and I will dwell in the house of the
LORD forever.
Ps. 23:4-6 NIV

YOU
preserve
me

Therefore, let everyone who is godly
pray to You in a time when You may
be found;
Surely in a flood of great waters
they will not reach him.
You are my hiding place;
You preserve me from trouble;
You surround me with songs of
deliverance. I will instruct you and
teach you in the way which you
should go;
I will counsel you with My eye upon
you. Do not be as the horse or as the
mule which have no understanding,
Whose trappings include bit and
bridle to hold them in check,
Otherwise they will not come near
to you. Many are the sorrows of the
wicked, But he who trusts in the
Lord, lovingkindness shall surround
him. Ps. 32:6-10 NASB

Yet God my King is from of old,
working salvation in the earth.   working
Ps. 74:12 NRSV   salvation

You clothed the earth with
floods of water,
water that covered even the mountains.
Then you set a firm boundary
for the seas,
so they would never again   NEVER AGAIN
cover the earth.
Ps. 104:6, 9 NLT

The LORD also will be a
stronghold for the oppressed,
A stronghold in times of trouble
Ps. 9:9 NASB

The poor
will eat and
be satisfied

The poor will eat and
be satisfied;
those who seek the LORD
will praise him…
Ps. 22:26 NIV

I know the LORD is
always with me.
I will not be shaken, for he
is right beside me. Ps. 16:8
NLT

YOU
repay all
people

Surely you repay all people
according to what they
have done.
Ps. 62:12 NLT

I HAVE BEEN

I called to the LORD, who is
worthy of praise, and I have
been saved from my enemies.
Ps. 18:3 NIV

S
A
V
E
D

The LORD preserves
the faithful
And fully recompenses the
proud doer.
Ps. 31:23 NASB

THE
LORD
PRESERVES

The LORD will keep you from all evil; he
will keep your life.
The LORD will keep
your going out and your coming in
from this time on and forevermore.
Ps. 121:7-8 NRSV

The
LORD
will keep
you from
all evil

For his anger lasts only a moment,
but his favor lasts a lifetime!
Weeping may last through the night,
but joy comes with the morning. You have
turned my mourning into joyful dancing.
You have taken away my clothes of
mourning and clothed me with joy, that I
might sing praises to you and not be silent.
O LORD my God,
I will give you thanks forever!
Ps. 30:5, 11-12 NLT

You will not
abandon my soul

For You will not abandon my soul to Sheol;
Nor will You allow Your Holy One to
undergo decay.
You will make known to me the path of life;
In Your presence is fullness of joy;
In Your right hand there are pleasures
forever.
Ps. 16:10-11 NASB

He will
give
justice
to the
poor

But I know the LORD
will help those they persecute;
he will give justice to the poor.
Surely righteous people
are praising your name;
the godly will live in your presence.
Ps. 140:12-13 NLT

The
HOPE
of the
poor

For the needy shall not always be forgotten,
nor the hope of the poor perish forever.
Ps. 9:18 NRSV

You,
LORD,
will keep the
needy safe

You, LORD, will keep the needy safe and will
protect us forever from the wicked...
Ps. 12:7 NIV

The LORD gives his people strength.
The LORD blesses them with peace.
Ps. 29:11 NLT

Only ask, and I will give you the nations as
your inheritance,
the whole earth as your possession.
Ps. 2:8 NLT

Behold, the eye of the LORD is on those who
fear Him,
On those who hope for His lovingkindness,
To deliver their soul from death
And to keep them alive in famine.
Ps. 33:18-19 NASB

He
will redeem
Israel

And He will redeem Israel
From all his iniquities. Ps. 130:8 NASB

Cast your burden upon the LORD
and He will sustain you;
He will never allow the righteous to be shaken.
But You, O God, will bring them
down to the pit of destruction;
Men of bloodshed and deceit will not live out half
their days... Ps. 55:22-23 NASB

He will sustain
you

Those who plant in tears
will harvest with shouts of joy.
They weep as they go to plant their seed,
but they sing as they return with the harvest.
Ps. 126:5-6 NLT

The earth has yielded its increase;
God, our God, has blessed us.
Ps. 67:6 NRSV

FOR
EVER
AND
EVER

Your throne, O God, endures forever and ever.
You rule with a scepter of justice. Ps. 45:6 NLT

He is mindful of his covenant forever,
of the word that he commanded,
for a thousand generations,
the covenant that he made with Abraham,
his sworn promise to Isaac,
which he confirmed to Jacob as a statute,
to Israel as an everlasting covenant,
saying, "To you I will give the land of Canaan
as your portion for an inheritance."
Ps. 105:8-11 NRSV

Unless the LORD builds the house,
They labor in vain who build it;
Unless the LORD guards the city,
The watchman keeps awake in vain. It
is vain for you to rise up early,
To retire late,
To eat the bread of painful labors;
For He gives to His beloved even in his
YOU   sleep. Ps. 127:1-2 NASB

D   You defend the orphans.
E   Ps. 10:14 NLT
F
E   The sacrifice acceptable to
E   God is a broken spirit;
N   a broken and contrite heart,
D   O God, you will not despise.
    Ps. 51:17 NRSV

With Your counsel
You will guide me,
And afterward receive me
to glory.
Ps. 73:24 NASB

RECEIVE ME TO
GLORY

You too are a Psalmist! Journal here, with dates…
You have experienced many of His promises. As His
steadfastness rocks your world, write of it.

A Psalmist Reveals God's Promises

_____

_____

_____

_____

_____

_____

_____

_____

_____

_____

_____

You too are a Psalmist! Journal here, with dates…
You have experienced many of His promises. As His
steadfastness rocks your world, write of it.

A Psalmist Reveals God's Promises

You too are a Psalmist! Journal here, with dates...
You have experienced many of His promises. As His
steadfastness rocks your world, write of it.

A Psalmist Reveals God's Promises

_____

_____

_____

_____

_____

_____

_____

_____

_____

_____

_____

You too are a Psalmist! Journal here, with dates...
You have experienced many of His promises. As His
steadfastness rocks your world, write of it.

A Psalmist Reveals God's Promises

_____

_____

_____

_____

_____

_____

_____

_____

_____

_____

_____

A Psalmist Praises Him

But you are a chosen people… that you may declare
the praises of him who called you out of darkness
into his wonderful light. 1 Peter 2:9 NIV

Shout joyfully to the LORD,
all the earth.
Serve the LORD with gladness;
Come before Him with joyful singing.
Enter His gates with thanksgiving
And His courts with praise...
Ps. 100:1-2, 4 NASB

THANKSGIVING

I will give to the LORD the thanks due
to his righteousness,
and sing praise to the name of the
LORD, the Most High.

I will
give thanks

Ps. 7:17 NRSV

I will sing of your love and justice, LORD.
I will praise you with songs.
Ps. 101:1 NLT

Then I will thank you
in the great congregation;
in the mighty throng I will praise you.
Then my tongue shall tell of your
righteousness and of your
praise all day long.
Ps. 35:18, 28 NRSV

The LORD reigns,
let the nations tremble…
Let them praise your great
and awesome name—
he is holy.
The King is mighty, he loves justice—
you have established equity;
in Jacob you have done
what is just and right.
Exalt the LORD our God
and worship at his footstool;
he is holy.
Exalt the LORD our God
and worship at his holy mountain,
for the LORD our God is holy.
Ps. 99:1, 3-5, 9 NIV

Worship at HIS footstool

Worship at HIS holy mountain

Therefore I will give thanks to You among
the nations, O LORD,
And I will sing praises to Your name.
He gives great deliverance to His king,
And shows lovingkindness to His
anointed,
To David and his descendants forever.
Ps. 18:49-50 NASB

I will give
thanks

I will tell

I will be glad

I will sing

I will give thanks to you, Lord, with all
my heart;
I will tell of all your wonderful deeds.
I will be glad and rejoice in you;
I will sing the praises of your name, O
Most High. The Lord reigns forever;
he has established his throne for judgment.
He rules the world in righteousness
and judges the peoples with equity.
Those who know your name trust in you,
for you, Lord, have never forsaken those
who seek you. Ps. 9:1-2, 7-8, 10 NIV

Make a joyful noise to God, all the earth;
sing the glory of his name;
give to him glorious praise.
Say to God, "How awesome are your deeds!
Because of your great power, your enemies
cringe before you.
All the earth worships you;
they sing praises to you,
sing praises to your name."
Come and see what God has done:
he is awesome in his deeds among mortals.
Bless our God, O peoples,
let the sound of his praise be heard
Ps. 66:1-5, 8 NRSV

COME
AND
SEE

Sing a new song to the LORD,
for he has done wonderful deeds.
His right hand has won a mighty victory;
his holy arm has shown his saving power!
The LORD has announced his victory
and has revealed his righteousness to every
nation! He has remembered his promise to
love and be faithful to Israel.
The ends of the earth have
seen the victory of our God.
Shout to the LORD, all the earth;
break out in praise and sing for joy!
Sing your praise to the
LORD with the harp,
with the harp and melodious song,
with trumpets and the sound of the ram's
horn. Make a joyful symphony before the
LORD, the King!
Let the sea and everything
in it shout his praise!
Let the earth and all living things join in.
Let the rivers clap their hands in glee!
Let the hills sing out their songs of joy
before the LORD.
For the LORD is coming to judge the earth.
He will judge the world with justice,
and the nations with fairness.
Ps. 98:1-9 NLT

Let the rivers clap their hands

Give thanks to the LORD, for he is good;
his love endures forever.
Shouts of joy and victory
resound in the tents of the righteous:
"The LORD's right hand has done mighty things!
The LORD's right hand is lifted high;

I will not
die but
L
I
V
E

the LORD's right hand has done mighty things!"
I will not die but live, and will proclaim what
the LORD has done.
I will give you thanks, for you answered me;
you have become my salvation.
The LORD is God,
and he has made his light shine on us...
You are my God, and I will praise you;
you are my God, and I will exalt you.
Give thanks to the LORD, for he is good;
his love endures forever.
Ps. 118:1, 15-17, 21, 27, 28-29 NIV

Praise is
becoming

Sing for joy in the LORD, O you righteous ones;
Praise is becoming to the upright.
Give thanks to the LORD with the lyre;
Sing praises to Him with a harp of ten strings.
Sing to Him a new song;
Play skillfully with a shout of joy.
Let all the earth fear the LORD;
Let all the inhabitants of the world stand in awe
of Him. Ps. 33:1-3, 8 NASB

Praise the LORD!
For it is good to sing praises to our God;
For it is pleasant and praise is becoming.
Sing to the LORD with thanksgiving;
Sing praises to our God on the lyre
Praise the LORD, O Jerusalem!
Praise your God, O Zion!   It is pleasant
Ps. 147:1, 7, 12 NASB

But I trust in your unfailing love.
I will rejoice because you have rescued me.
I will sing to the LORD
because he is good to me.
Ps. 13:5-6 NLT

Sing praises to the LORD, O you his   Sing
faithful ones, and give thanks to his holy   Praises
name. Ps. 30:4 NRSV

Clap your hands, all you peoples;   CLAP
shout to God with loud songs of joy.
Sing praises to God, sing praises;   SING
sing praises to our King, sing praises.
Ps. 47:1, 6 NRSV

Praise the LORD!
Sing to the LORD a new song,
And His praise in the congregation of the
godly ones.
Let Israel be glad in his Maker;
Let the sons of Zion rejoice in their King.
Let them praise His name with dancing;
Let them sing praises to Him with timbrel
and lyre.
For the LORD takes pleasure in His people;
He will beautify the afflicted ones with
salvation.
Let the godly ones exult in glory;
Let them sing for joy on their beds.
Let the high praises of God be in their
mouth,
And a two-edged sword in their hand,
To execute vengeance on the nations
And punishment on the peoples,
To bind their kings with chains
And their nobles with fetters of iron,
To execute on them the judgment written;
This is an honor for all His godly ones.
Praise the LORD!
Ps. 149:1-9 NASB

Sing to the
LORD
a new song

Sing praises to God and to his name!
Sing loud praises to him who rides the
clouds. His name is the LORD—
rejoice in his presence!
Praise the LORD; praise God our savior!
For each day he carries us in his arms.
Praise God, all you people of Israel; praise
the LORD, the source of Israel's life.
Sing to the one who rides
across the ancient heavens,
his mighty voice thundering from the sky.
Tell everyone about God's power.
His majesty shines down on Israel;
his strength is mighty in the heavens.
God is awesome in his sanctuary.
The God of Israel gives power and strength
to his people.
Praise be to God!
Ps. 68:4, 19, 26, 33-35 NLT

My heart exults

in him my heart trusts;
so I am helped, and my heart exults,
and with my song I give thanks to him.
Ps. 28:7 NRSV

We praise
You
For
Your Name is
near

We praise you, God,
we praise you, for your Name is near;
people tell of your wonderful deeds.
As for me, I will declare this forever;
I will sing praise to the God of Jacob,
who says, "I will cut off the horns of all the wicked,
but the horns of the righteous will be lifted up."
Ps. 75:1, 9-10 NIV

Sing aloud to God our strength;
shout for joy to the God of Jacob.
Raise a song, sound the tambourine,
the sweet lyre with the harp.
Blow the trumpet at the new moon,
at the full moon, on our festal day.
For it is a statute for Israel,
an ordinance of the God of Jacob.
Ps. 81:1-4 NRSV

Wake up, my heart!
Wake up, O lyre and harp!
I will wake the dawn with my song.
Ps. 57:8 NLT

With my dying
breath

Praise the LORD!
Let all that I am praise the LORD.
I will praise the LORD as long as I live.
I will sing praises to my God with my dying breath.
Ps. 146:1-2 NLT

I will give You thanks with all my heart;
I will sing praises to You before the gods.
I will bow down toward Your holy temple
And give thanks to Your name for Your
lovingkindness and Your truth;
For You have magnified Your word according to
all Your name.
On the day I called, You answered me;
You made me bold with strength in my soul.
All the kings of the earth will give thanks to You,
O Lord,
When they have heard the words of Your mouth.
And they will sing of the ways of the Lord,
For great is the glory of the Lord.
Ps. 138:1-5 NASB

I will thank
YOU
among all
the people

My heart is confident in you, O God;
no wonder I can sing your
praises with all my heart!
Wake up, lyre and harp!
I will wake the dawn with my song.
I will thank you, Lord, among all the people.
I will sing your praises among the nations.
For your unfailing love is higher than the heavens.
Your faithfulness reaches to the clouds.
Be exalted, O God, above the highest heavens.
May your glory shine over all the earth.
Ps. 108:1-5 NLT

Be glad in the Lord and rejoice, O righteous,
and shout for joy, all you upright in heart.
Ps. 32:11 NRSV

It is good to praise the LORD
and make music to your name, O Most High,
proclaiming your love in the morning
and your faithfulness at night,
to the music of the ten-stringed lyre
and the melody of the harp.
For you make me glad by your deeds, LORD;
I sing for joy at what your hands have done.
You have exalted my horn like that of a wild ox;
fine oils have been poured on me.
My eyes have seen the defeat of my adversaries;
my ears have heard the rout of my wicked foes.
The righteous will flourish like a palm tree,
they will grow like a cedar of Lebanon;
planted in the house of the LORD,
they will flourish in the courts of our God.
They will still bear fruit in old age,
they will stay fresh and green,
proclaiming, "The LORD is upright;
he is my Rock, and there is no wickedness in him."
Ps. 92:1-4, 10-15 NIV

I sing for joy at what YOUR hands have done

Praise the LORD!
I will give thanks to the LORD with all my heart,
In the company of the upright and in the assembly.
Ps. 111:1 NASB

I will extol you, my God and King,
and bless your name forever and ever.
Every day I will bless you,
and praise your name forever and ever.
Great is the Lord,
and greatly to be praised;
his greatness is unsearchable.
One generation shall
laud your works to another,
and shall declare your mighty acts.
On the glorious splendor of your majesty,
and on your wondrous works,
I will meditate.
The might of your awesome
deeds shall be proclaimed,
and I will declare your greatness.
They shall celebrate the fame of your
abundant goodness,
and shall sing aloud of your righteousness.
My mouth will speak
the praise of the Lord,
and all flesh will bless his holy name
forever and ever.
Ps. 145:1-7, 21 NRSV

Declare your
mighty
acts

Praise the LORD!
Praise God in his sanctuary;
praise him in his mighty firmament!
Praise him for his mighty deeds;
praise him according
to his surpassing greatness!
Praise him with trumpet sound;
praise him with lute and harp!
Praise him with tambourine and dance;
praise him with strings and pipe!
Praise him with clanging cymbals;
praise him with loud clashing cymbals!
Let everything that breathes praise the
LORD! Praise the LORD!
Ps. 150:1-6 NRSV

There I will go to the altar of God,
to God—the source of all my joy.
I will praise you with my harp,
O God, my God!
Why am I discouraged?
Why is my heart so sad?
I will put my hope in God!
I will praise him again—
my Savior and my God!
Ps. 43:4, 5 NLT

O LORD my God, you have performed
many wonders for us.
Your plans for us are too numerous to list.
You have no equal.
If I tried to recite all your wonderful deeds,
I would never come to the end of them.
Ps. 40:5 NLT

I will bless the LORD at all times;
His praise shall continually
be in my mouth.
My soul will make its boast in the LORD;
The humble will hear it and rejoice.
O magnify the LORD with me,
And let us exalt His name together.
I sought the LORD, and He answered me,
And delivered me from all my fears.
Ps. 34:1-4 NASB

I sought
the LORD

But I will give repeated thanks to the
LORD, praising him to everyone.
For he stands beside the needy,
ready to save them from those who
condemn them.
Ps. 109:30-31 NLT

I will sing of the LORD's great love forever;
with my mouth I will make
your faithfulness known
through all generations.
I will declare that your love stands firm
forever, that you have established your
faithfulness in heaven itself.
Ps. 89:1-2 NIV

With my
mouth I will
make YOUR
faithfulness
known

I give thanks to you, O LORD my God,
with my whole heart,
and I will glorify your name forever.
Ps. 86:12 NRSV

Praise the LORD, the God of Israel,
who lives from everlasting to everlasting.
Amen and amen! Ps. 41:13 NLT

Praise the
LORD, my
soul.

Praise the LORD, my soul.
LORD my God, you are very great;
you are clothed with splendor and majesty.
Ps. 104:1 NIV

Bless the LORD, O my soul,
and all that is within me,
bless his holy name.
Bless the LORD, O my soul,
and do not forget all his benefits—
Bless the LORD, O you his angels,
you mighty ones who do his bidding,
obedient to his spoken word.
Bless the LORD, all his hosts,
his ministers that do his will.
Bless the LORD, all his works,
in all places of his dominion.
Bless the LORD, O my soul.
Ps. 103:1-2, 20-22 NRSV

*from
everlasting
to
everlasting*

Praise the LORD!
Give thanks to the LORD, for he is good!
His faithful love endures forever.
Who can list the glorious miracles of the LORD?
Who can ever praise him enough?
Praise the LORD, the God of Israel,
who lives from everlasting to everlasting...
Ps. 106:1-2, 48 NLT

Praise the LORD! Praise, O servants of the LORD,
Praise the name of the LORD.
Blessed be the name of the LORD
From this time forth and forever.
From the rising of the sun to its setting
The name of the LORD is to be praised.
Ps. 113:1-3 NASB

*from the rising
of the sun*

Praise the LORD,
who did not let their teeth tear us apart!
We escaped like a bird from a hunter's trap.
The trap is broken, and we are free!
Our help is from the LORD, who made
heaven and earth. Ps. 124:6-8 NLT

Our help
is from
the LORD,
who made
heaven and
earth.

F
O
R
E
V
E
R

I will exalt you, LORD, for you rescued me.
You refused to let my enemies triumph over
me. O LORD my God, I cried to you for
help, and you restored my health.
I will give you thanks forever!
Ps. 30:1-2, 12 NLT

Praise the LORD, all you nations!
Extol him, all you peoples!
For great is his steadfast love toward us,
and the faithfulness of
the LORD endures forever.
Praise the LORD! Ps. 117:1-2 NRSV

My
ROCK

Blessed be the LORD, my rock,
who trains my hands for war, and my
fingers for battle; my rock and my fortress,
my stronghold and my deliverer, my shield,
in whom I take refuge, who subdues the
peoples under me.
Ps. 144:1-2 NRSV

I love your sanctuary, LORD,
the place where your
glorious presence dwells.
Now I stand on solid ground,
and I will publicly praise the LORD.
Ps. 26:8, 12 NLT

I will publicly praise

Behold, bless the LORD, all servants of the
LORD, Who serve by night in the house of
the LORD! Lift up your
hands to the sanctuary
And bless the LORD. May the LORD bless
you from Zion, He who made heaven and
earth.
Ps. 134:1-3 NASB

I was glad when they said to me,
"Let us go to the house of the LORD!"
Our feet are standing
within your gates, O Jerusalem.
Jerusalem—built as a city
that is bound firmly together.
To it the tribes go up,
the tribes of the LORD,
as was decreed for Israel,
to give thanks to the name of the LORD.
Ps. 122:1-4 NRSV

Praise the LORD!
Praise the LORD from the heavens;
Praise Him in the heights!
Praise Him, all His angels;
Praise Him, all His hosts!
Praise Him, sun and moon;
Praise Him, all stars of light!
Praise Him, highest heavens,
And the waters that are above the heavens!
Let them praise the name of the LORD,
For He commanded and they were created.
He has also established them forever and ever;
He has made a decree which will not pass away.
Praise the LORD from the earth,
Sea monsters and all deePs.;
Fire and hail, snow and clouds;
Stormy wind, fulfilling His word;
Mountains and all hills;
Fruit trees and all cedars;
Beasts and all cattle;
Creeping things and winged fowl;
Kings of the earth and all peoples;
Princes and all judges of the earth;
Both young men and virgins;
Old men and children.
Let them praise the name of the LORD,
For His name alone is exalted;
His glory is above earth and heaven.
And He has lifted up a horn for His people,
Praise for all His godly ones;
Even for the sons of Israel, a people near to Him.
Praise the LORD!
Ps. 148:1-14 NASB

I lift up my eyes to you,
to you who sit enthroned in heaven.
As the eyes of slaves look
to the hand of their master,
as the eyes of a female slave look to the
hand of her mistress,
so our eyes look to the LORD our God,
till he shows us his mercy.
Ps. 123:1-2 NIV

I WILL
LIFT
MY EYES
TO YOU

Serve the LORD with reverent fear,
and rejoice with trembling.
Submit to God's royal son,
or he will become angry,
and you will be destroyed in the midst of
all your activities—
for his anger flares up in an instant.
But what joy for all who
take refuge in him!
Ps. 2:11-12 NLT

Honor the LORD, you heavenly beings;
honor the LORD for his glory and strength.
Honor the LORD for the glory of his name.
Worship the LORD in the
splendor of his holiness.
Ps. 29:1-2 NLT

LORD,
not to us but
to YOUR
name goes
all the
glory

Offer to God a sacrifice of
thanksgiving,
and pay your vows to the Most High.
Call on me in the day of trouble;
I will deliver you, and
you shall glorify me."
Ps. 50: 14-15 NRSV

Not to us, O LORD, not to us,
but to your name goes all the glory
for your unfailing love and
faithfulness.
Ps. 115:1 NLT

O give thanks to the LORD,
for he is good;
for his steadfast love endures forever.
Ps. 107:1 NRSV

O LORD, our Sovereign,
how majestic is your
name in all the earth!
When I look at your heavens,
the work of your fingers,
the moon and the stars that
you have established;
what are human beings that
you are mindful of them,
mortals that you care for them?
Ps. 8:1, 3-4 NRSV

GIVE
THANKS

Give thanks to the LORD,
for he is good!
His faithful love endures forever.
Give thanks to the God of gods.
His faithful love endures forever.
Give thanks to the LORD of lords.
His faithful love endures forever.
Ps. 136:1-3 NLT

You too are a Psalmist! Journal here, with dates…
You acknowledge Him as the Author of all things good.
Journal your thoughts of praise.

A Psalmist Praises Him

_____

_____

_____

_____

_____

_____

_____

_____

_____

_____

_____

_____

You too are a Psalmist! Journal here, with dates...
You acknowledge Him as the Author of all things good.
Journal your thoughts of praise.

A Psalmist Praises Him

You too are a Psalmist! Journal here, with dates…
You acknowledge Him as the Author of all things good.
Journal your thoughts of praise.

A Psalmist Praises Him

_____

_____

_____

_____

_____

_____

_____

_____

_____

_____

_____

_____

You too are a Psalmist! Journal here, with dates...
You acknowledge Him as the Author of all things good.
Journal your thoughts of praise.

A Psalmist Praises Him

_____

_____

_____

_____

_____

_____

_____

_____

_____

_____

_____

_____

A Psalmist Points to Christ

"I know that Messiah" (called Christ) "is coming..."
John 4:25 NIV

Oh, that salvation for Israel would
come out of Zion!
When the LORD restores his people,
let Jacob rejoice and Israel be glad!
Ps. 14:7 NIV

Oh, that
salvation
would
come!

Malicious witnesses rise up;
they ask me about things I do not know.
Ps. 35:11 NRSV

Oh, that the salvation of Israel would
come out of Zion...
Ps. 53:6 NASB

Oh, that
salvation
would
come

Even my close friend in whom I trusted,
Who ate my bread,
Has lifted up his heel against me.
Ps. 41:9 NASB

'You are my son.
Today I have become your Father...'
Ps. 2:7 NLT

you will not abandon me to
the realm of the dead,
nor will you let your
faithful one see decay.
Ps. 16:10 NIV

The stone that the builders rejected
has now become the cornerstone.
The
cornerstone

This is the LORD's doing,
and it is wonderful to see.
This is the day the LORD has made.
We will rejoice and be glad in it.
Please, LORD, please save us.
Please, LORD, please give us success.

LORD,
Please save us!

Bless the one who comes in
the name of the LORD.
We bless you from the house of the LORD.
Ps. 118:22-26 NLT

My God, my God, why have you
forsaken me...
All who see me mock me;
they hurl insults, shaking their heads.
"He trusts in the LORD," they say, "let
the LORD rescue him.
Let him deliver him,
since he delights in him."
I am poured out like water,
and all my bones are out of joint.
My heart has turned to wax;
it has melted within me.
My mouth is dried up like a potsherd,
and my tongue sticks
to the roof of my mouth;
you lay me in the dust of death
they pierce my hands and my feet.
All my bones are on display;
people stare and gloat over me.
They divide my clothes among them
and cast lots for my garment.
Ps. 22:1, 7-8, 14-15, 16, 17-18 NIV

I am poured out like water

You
brought
a vine
out of Egypt

You brought a vine out of Egypt;
you drove out the nations
and planted it.
You cleared the ground for it;
it took deep root and filled the land.
The mountains were
covered with its shade,
the mighty cedars with its branches;
it sent out its branches to the sea,
and its shoots to the River.
Why then have you
broken down its walls,
so that all who pass along the way
pluck its fruit?
The boar from the forest ravages it,

and all that move in the field feed on it.
Turn again, O God of hosts;
look down from heaven,
and see; have regard for this vine,
the stock that your
right hand planted.

Have regard for this vine

They have burned it with fire,
they have cut it down;
may they perish at
the rebuke of your countenance.
But let your hand be upon the one at
your right hand,
the one whom you
made strong for yourself.

They have cut it down

Then we will never turn back from
you; give us life, and we will call on
your name.
Ps. 80:8-18 NRSV

Sacrifice and offering you did
not desire—
but my ears you have
opened—
burnt offerings and sin
offerings you did not require.
Then I said,
"Here I am, I have come—
it is written   it is written about me
about me   in the scroll.
I desire to do your will,
my God;
your law is within my heart."
Ps. 40:6-8 NIV

For zeal for Your house
has consumed me,
And the reproaches of those who
reproach You have fallen on me.
They also gave me gall for my food
And for my thirst they gave me
vinegar to drink.
Ps. 69:9, 21 NASB

Your throne, O God,
will last for ever and ever;
a scepter of justice will
be the scepter of your kingdom.
You love righteousness
and hate wickedness;
therefore God, your God, has set you
above your companions
by anointing you with the oil of joy.
Ps. 45:6-7 NIV

by anointing
you with the
oil of JOY

The LORD has sworn and will
not change His mind,
"You are a priest forever
According to the order of
Melchizedek."
Ps. 110:4 NASB

I will establish your seed forever
And build up your throne to all
generations."
Ps. 89:4 NASB

For the LORD protects the bones
of the righteous;
not one of them is broken!
Ps. 34:20 NLT

Into Your hand I commit my
spirit…
Ps. 31:5 NASB

Long ago you laid the
foundation of the earth,
and the heavens are the
work of your hands.
They will perish, but you endure;
they will all wear out like a garment.
You change them like clothing, and
they pass away;
but you are the same,
and your years have no end.
Ps. 102:25-27 NRSV

LONG AGO

Your years have
no end

You too are a Psalmist! Journal here, with dates…
We, today, have the benefit of living daily with Christ
in our lives. Journal how you are living in that truth.

A Psalmist Points to Christ

_____

_____

_____

_____

_____

_____

_____

_____

_____

_____

_____

_____

You too are a Psalmist! Journal here, with dates…
We, today, have the benefit of living daily with Christ
in our lives. Journal how you are living in that truth.

A Psalmist Points to Christ

You too are a Psalmist! Journal here, with dates…
We, today, have the benefit of living daily with Christ
in our lives. Journal how you are living in that truth.

A Psalmist Points to Christ

_____

_____

_____

_____

_____

_____

_____

_____

_____

_____

_____

You too are a Psalmist! Journal here, with dates…
We, today, have the benefit of living daily with Christ
in our lives. Journal how you are living in that truth.

A Psalmist Points to Christ

_____

_____

_____

_____

_____

_____

_____

_____

_____

_____

_____

_____

A Psalmist Recounts God's Ways

"Great and marvelous are your deeds, LORD God Almighty.
Just and true are your ways, King of the nations."
Revelation 15:3 NIV

By the word of the LORD
the heavens were made,
And by the breath of
His mouth all their host.
He gathers the waters of
the sea together as a heap...
For He spoke, and it was done;   He spoke
He commanded, and it stood fast.
The LORD nullifies the
counsel of the nations;
He frustrates the plans of the peoples.
The counsel of the LORD stands forever,
The plans of His heart from
generation to generation.
Ps. 33:6-7, 9-11 NASB

You divided the sea by your might;
you broke the heads of the
dragons in the waters.
You crushed the heads of Leviathan;

You
made
summer
and
winter

you gave him as food for
the creatures of the wilderness.
You cut openings for
  springs and torrents;
you dried up ever-flowing streams.
Yours is the day, yours also the night;
you established the
luminaries and the sun.
You have fixed all the bounds of the earth;
you made summer and winter.
Ps. 74:13-17 NRSV

When God went out against Egypt,
he established it as a statute for Joseph.
I heard an unknown voice say:
I removed the burden from their shoulders;
their hands were set free from the basket.
In your distress you
called and I rescued you,
I answered you out of a thundercloud;
I tested you at the waters of Meribah.
"But my people would not listen to me;
Israel would not submit to me.
So I gave them over to
their stubborn hearts
to follow their own devices.
"If my people would only listen to me,
if Israel would only follow my ways,
how quickly I would subdue their enemies
and turn my hand against their foes!
Those who hate the LORD
would cringe before him,
and their punishment would last forever.
But you would be fed with the finest of
wheat; with honey from the rock I would
satisfy you."
Ps. 81:5-7, 11-16 NIV

For the LORD has
chosen Jacob for himself,
Israel for his own special treasure.
He destroyed the firstborn in each
Egyptian home,
both people and animals.

HE
performed
miraculous
signs

He performed miraculous signs and
wonders in Egypt
against Pharaoh and all his people.
He struck down great nations
and slaughtered mighty kings—
Sihon king of the Amorites,
Og king of Bashan,
and all the kings of Canaan.
He gave their land as an inheritance,
a special possession to his people Israel.
Ps. 135:4, 8-12 NLT

Come and see what God has done:
he is awesome in his
deeds among mortals.
He turned the sea into dry land;
they passed through the river on foot.
There we rejoiced in him,   YOU brought
who rules by his might forever,   us out to a
whose eyes keep   spacious
watch on the nations—   place
let the rebellious not exalt themselves.
For you, O God, have tested us;
you have tried us as silver is tried.
You brought us into the net;
you laid burdens on our backs;
you let people ride over our heads;
we went through fire and through water;
yet you have brought us out to a
spacious place.
But truly God has listened;
he has given heed to the words of my
prayer.
Ps. 66:5-7, 10-12, 19 NRSV

Your way, O God, is holy.

What god is so great as our God?

You are the God who works wonders;

the GOD   you have displayed your

who   might among the peoples.

works   With your strong arm

wonders   you redeemed your people,

the descendants of Jacob and Joseph.

Your way was through the sea,

your path, through the mighty waters;

yet your footprints were unseen. You

led your people like a flock by the

hand of Moses and Aaron.

Yet

YOUR   Ps. 77:13-15, 19-20 NRSV

footprints

were unseen

When Israel went forth from Egypt,
The house of Jacob from a people of
strange language,
Judah became His sanctuary,
Israel, His dominion.
The sea looked and fled;
The Jordan turned back.
The mountains skipped like rams,
The hills, like lambs.
What ails you, O sea, that you flee?
O Jordan, that you turn back?
O mountains,
that you skip like rams?
O hills, like lambs?
Tremble, O earth, before the LORD,
Before the God of Jacob,
Who turned the rock
into a pool of water,
The flint into a fountain of water.
Ps. 114:1-8 NASB

who turned the
rock into a pool
of water

Let the redeemed of the Lord tell their

story…

They were hungry and thirsty,

and their lives ebbed away.

Then they cried out to

the Lord in their trouble,

and   and he delivered them from their distress.

HE   He led them by a straight way

delivered   to a city where they could settle.

them   Some sat in darkness, in utter darkness,

from their   prisoners suffering in iron chains,

distress   because they rebelled

against God's commands

and despised the plans of the Most High.

So he subjected them to bitter labor;

they stumbled, and there was no one to help.

Then they cried to the

Lord in their trouble,

and he saved them from their distress.

He brought them out of darkness, the utter

darkness, and broke away their chains.

Some became fools through

their rebellious ways

and suffered affliction

because of their iniquities.

They loathed all food

and drew near the gates of death.
Then they cried to the
Lord in their trouble,
and he saved them from their distress.
He sent out his word and healed them;
he rescued them from the grave.
He turned rivers into a desert,
flowing springs into thirsty ground,
and fruitful land into a salt waste,
because of the wickedness of
those who lived there.
He turned the desert into pools of water
and the parched ground
into flowing springs;
there he brought the hungry to live,
and they founded a city where they could
settle. Then their numbers decreased,
and they were humbled
by oppression, calamity and sorrow;
he who pours contempt on nobles
made them wander in a trackless waste.
But he lifted the needy out of their affliction
and increased their families like flocks.
Ps. 107:2, 5-7, 10-14, 17-20, 33-36, 39-41
NIV

but
HE
Lifted
the needy
out
of
their
affliction

O give thanks to the LORD, for he is good,
for his steadfast love endures forever.
O give thanks to the God of gods,
for his steadfast love endures forever.
O give thanks to the LORD of lords,
for his steadfast love endures forever;
who alone does great wonders,
for his steadfast love endures forever;
who by understanding made the heavens,
for his steadfast love endures forever;
who spread out the earth on the waters,
for his steadfast love endures forever;
who made the great lights,
for his steadfast love endures forever;
the sun to rule over the day,
for his steadfast love endures forever;
the moon and stars to rule over the night,
for his steadfast love endures forever;
who struck Egypt through their firstborn,
for his steadfast love endures forever;
and brought Israel out from among them,
for his steadfast love endures forever;

with a strong hand and
an outstretched arm,
for his steadfast love endures forever;
who divided the Red Sea in two,
for his steadfast love endures forever;
and made Israel pass through
the midst of it,
for his steadfast love endures forever;
but overthrew Pharaoh and his army in the
Red Sea,
for his steadfast love endures forever;
who led his people through the wilderness,
for his steadfast love endures forever;
who struck down great kings,
for his steadfast love endures forever;
and killed famous kings,
for his steadfast love endures forever;
Sihon, king of the Amorites,
for his steadfast love endures forever;
and Og, king of Bashan,
for his steadfast love endures forever;
and gave their land as a heritage,
for his steadfast love endures forever;
a heritage to his servant Israel,
for his steadfast love endures forever.

It is he who remembered
us in our low estate,
for his steadfast love endures forever;
and rescued us from our foes,
for his steadfast love endures forever;
who gives food to all flesh,
for his steadfast love endures forever.
O give thanks to the God of heaven,
for his steadfast love endures forever.
Ps. 136:1-26 NRSV

Psalmist,
I Am

HIS
STEADFAST
LOVE ENDURES
FOREVER

You too are a Psalmist! Journal here, with dates…
You have seen His handiworks! Tell of all the great
things He has done in your life!

A Psalmist Recounts God's Ways

_____

_____

_____

_____

_____

_____

_____

_____

_____

_____

_____

You too are a Psalmist! Journal here, with dates…
You have seen His handiworks! Tell of all the great
things He has done in your life!

A Psalmist Recounts God's Ways

_____

_____

_____

_____

_____

_____

_____

_____

_____

_____

_____

_____

You too are a Psalmist! Journal here, with dates...
You have seen His handiworks! Tell of all the great
things He has done in your life!
A Psalmist Recounts God's Ways

_____

_____

_____

_____

_____

_____

_____

_____

_____

_____

_____

You too are a Psalmist! Journal here, with dates…
You have seen His handiworks! Tell of all the great
things He has done in your life!

A Psalmist Recounts God's Ways

_____

_____

_____

_____

_____

_____

_____

_____

_____

_____

_____

Psalm Index

Ps. 1 101, 113, 140

Ps. 2 100, 113, 180, 209, 218

Ps. 3 5, 54, 171

Ps. 4 42, 171

Ps. 5 13, 42, 116, 118, 172

Ps. 6 43, 118, 171

Ps. 7 5, 46, 190

Ps. 8 211

Ps. 9 6, 46, 115, 175, 179, 192

Ps. 10 11, 44, 182

Ps. 11 14, 121, 172

Ps. 12 15, 117, 180

Ps. 13 60, 195

Ps. 14 9, 123, 217

Ps. 15 141

Ps. 16 6, 63, 122, 139, 176, 179, 218

Ps. 17 39, 47, 119, 152

Ps. 18 16, 73, 144, 177, 191

Ps. 19 15, 43

Ps. 20 44, 169

Ps. 21 57, 124

Ps. 22 44, 72, 142, 170, 176, 219

Ps. 23 9, 173

Ps. 24 3, 139

Ps. 25 16, 50, 116, 143

Ps. 26 56, 140, 207

Ps. 27 7, 149

Ps. 28 6, 53, 124, 197

Ps. 29 180, 209

Ps. 30 72, 178, 195, 206

Ps. 31 92, 177, 224

Ps. 32 14, 102, 142, 174, 199

Ps. 33 39, 103, 145, 180, 194, 231

Ps. 34 148, 203, 224

Ps. 35 21, 74, 190, 217

Ps. 36 8, 47, 118

Ps. 37 120, 144

Ps. 38 60, 77, 171

Ps. 39 54, 78

Ps. 40 4, 53, 103, 151, 203, 222

Ps. 41 42, 79, 104, 137, 204, 218

Ps. 42 81

Ps. 43 4, 52, 82, 202

Ps. 44 18, 58, 82, 156

Ps. 45 56, 181, 223

Ps. 46 17

Ps. 47 21, 195

Ps. 48 17, 124, 140

Ps. 49 125, 172

Ps. 50 115, 210

Ps. 51 152, 182

Ps. 52 119, 140
Ps. 53 128, 217
Ps. 54 14, 84, 160
Ps. 55 18, 57, 83, 145, 181
Ps. 56 59, 154
Ps. 57 40, 127, 154, 198
Ps. 58 41, 131
Ps. 59 45, 85, 153
Ps. 60 56
Ps. 61 58, 153
Ps. 62 10, 84, 127, 155, 176
Ps. 63 14, 150
Ps. 64 130, 170
Ps. 65 23, 99
Ps. 66 192, 235
Ps. 67 40, 181
Ps. 68 23, 58, 130, 197
Ps. 69 13, 55, 90, 159, 223
Ps. 70 59
Ps. 71 5, 50, 129, 138
Ps. 72 19, 45, 100
Ps. 73 13, 114, 159, 183
Ps. 74 52, 175, 232
Ps. 75 198
Ps. 77 88, 236
Ps. 78 155
Ps. 79 86
Ps. 80 63, 87, 221
Ps. 81 13, 198, 233
Ps. 82 24, 62, 123
Ps. 83 57, 117
Ps. 84 24, 63, 100
Ps. 85 19, 62
Ps. 86 22, 51, 122, 170, 204
Ps. 88 3, 88
Ps. 89 25, 106, 204, 224
Ps. 90 61, 93
Ps. 92 7, 200
Ps. 93 10

Ps. 94 12, 106, 126
Ps. 95 10
Ps. 98 193
Ps. 99 191
Ps. 100 7, 189
Ps. 101 190
Ps. 102 32, 63, 75, 157, 225
Ps. 103 20, 205
Ps. 104 27, 160, 175, 204
Ps. 105 8, 181
Ps. 106 18, 61, 102, 142, 205
Ps. 107 158, 210, 239
Ps. 108 199
Ps. 109 55, 203
Ps. 110 224
Ps. 111 10, 200
Ps. 112 103, 113, 158
Ps. 113 12, 205
Ps. 114 237
Ps. 115 121, 161, 210
Ps. 116 89
Ps. 117 206
Ps. 118 89, 102, 143, 194, 218
Ps. 119 9, 30, 49, 90, 107, 129, 147
Ps. 120 91
Ps. 121 178
Ps. 122 64, 207
Ps. 123 84, 209
Ps. 124 206
Ps. 125 131, 157
Ps. 126 156, 181
Ps. 127 105, 182
Ps. 128 107
Ps. 129 128
Ps. 130 13, 71, 149, 180
Ps. 131 161
Ps. 133 162
Ps. 134 207
Ps. 135 33, 116, 234

Ps. 136 211, 242
Ps. 137 91
Ps. 138 12, 199
Ps. 139 29, 41, 129
Ps. 140 179
Ps. 141 51
Ps. 142 73
Ps. 144 46, 99, 206
Ps. 145 31, 201
Ps. 146 11, 105, 145, 198
Ps. 147 195
Ps. 148 208
Ps. 149 196
Ps. 150 202

Interesting how we experience such waves of emotion and thought. Many Christians, perhaps, feel as if this is not appropriate. The Psalms show it differently. The psalmists certainly share many changing emotions in their writings! Here is a truth about God that is hard to grab hold of...

He understands! To experience various waves of emotion is OK!

Journal your thoughts – be a psalmist!

—Ray Abner

Psalmist,

I Am

The psalmists wear their thoughts and emotions 'on their sleeves'...

You share many of these same emotions, don't you? You are like a Psalmist!

Psalmist, I Am will be helpful as your daily devotion, a Bible study aid, for journaling or as a gift for anyone who experiences emotional change in their relationship! May **Psalmist, I Am** stir your soul as you realize how much you have in common with the writers of the Psalms!